Transforming
The Minds of Men:
Maximizing Potential
from Childhood to Manhood

Lovelle McMichael

Dedication

T his book is dedicated to my grandfather, Henry Schley. My grandfather is a trailblazer and a part of Philadelphia's unwritten history. He began a grassroots barber and beauty salon in the 1950's in order to provide economic development, employment, and style to African-American men and women. He is a family man and strong patriarch. His enduring sense of family, business, and helping others is the foundation of all I have accomplished in life. My grandfather taught me how to be a businessman and responsible father. These are two intangible gifts for which I am forever grateful.

I would also like to dedicate this book to the men who played major roles in my maturation into a successful black man: Ronald Harris, Eric McMichael Sr., David Edwards, Timothy Smith, and Apostle Kenneth Porter. At different points in my life, these men fathered me and served as role models during my journey of self-discovery and discovering my passion.

My sons, Lovelle Jr. and Logan, will be the beneficiaries of any legacy I am permitted to establish, and I love them unconditionally. I have also mentored several young black men, Ashton Moyer, Daryl Mills, and Kedrick Mitchell, whom have taught me the value of a male presence in the life of a young male. This book is dedicated to all young men who have been fatherless and those men who are present in the lives of young men as fathers or father figures, empowering them to be the best they can be.

• • •

Acknowledgements

I am grateful that I have been afforded experiences that allow me to share the need for transformation and recognizing my own untapped potential in order to maximize the quality and enjoyment of life. I am excited to provide my education, experience, and application of the tools and strategies I have learned with the world.

I am delighted to begin my journey as an author with Lavon Lewis and Sherrod Shackelford of PDGbranding.com (formerly Pencilworx Design Group) and Anthony Parnell of the Fatherhood Support Network. These men have been instrumental in my journey of discovering and maximizing my personal potential in an area that I could only dream. Turning Point Youth Facility and Impacted for Purpose have provided me with years of practical application of the tools and strategies that I have shared with the readers of this book.

Connie Drake Wilson has pulled the best out of me by challenging my writing. Thank you for editing my work and making sure it was technical and met the standards of academia. My extra set of eyes on this project have been amazing.

Thank you Shariff McMichael, Dr. Angie Williams-McMichael, and Carol Parker for editing chapters as I completed them and providing me real-time and real life feedback. It was not always easy to endure such a high level of scrutiny, but the process helped me to better articulate the message of hope and promise that I am sending to young black males. I thank Dr. Matthew Whitaker, Brother Mark S. Tillman, Vickie Winans, and Ricky Dillard for believing in the promise of this black man and the black males in communities throughout America.

Additionally, I would like to thank The Delta Tau Lambda Chapter of Alpha Phi Alpha Fraternity, Incorporated, The State of Black Arizona, the cities of Phoenix and Mesa, AZ for your continued support as I provide services to the most vulnerable youth in the state.

Lastly, but certainly not least, I thank my wife and sons who have been my driving force. Thank you for making countless sacrifices in an effort to support my passion for serving the community and this project.

• • •

Contents

Dedication 5

Acknowledgements..7

Foreword..11

Introduction 16

Chapter 1: Beating the Odds 19

Chapter 2: Fatherlessness 35

Chapter 3: Words I Wish My Father Had Spoken to Me................53

Chapter 4: Self-Discovery.................................... 69

Chapter 5: Move..89

Chapter 6: Relationships......................................109

Chapter 7: Mentoring 129

Chapter 8: Coping With No....................................143

Chapter 9: No Excuses..157

Chapter 10: A Life Worth Living............................171

Conclusion 179

References 187

About the Author 193

Foreword

This book is not only an illuminating and timely contribution to the growing body of literature about the status and future of Black men in America, it is also a highly accessible and inspirational literary. The social construction of race and equality is at the forefront of our national consciousness, and there is a compelling and evolving dialogue surrounding fatherlessness, particularly of African American males, and its effects their education, career, relationships, and quality of life. Transforming the Minds of Men: Maximizing Potential from Childhood to Manhood is a welcomed addition in the discussion on how to remedy the negative impacts of absentee fathers.

Lovelle A. McMichael Sr. is a respected leader in education, child welfare advocacy, and mentoring, with more than 15 years of experience. The work to which Lovelle has placed his hands speaks to his unending commitment to making the world a better place. His labors are making an impact not only in his local community, but around the globe. He is committed to addressing people's needs holistically so they can improve mentally, spiritually, emotionally, physically, and intellectually.

He continues to be a strong advocate for educational equality and for youth ensnared in the juvenile justice system. He is a rising voice for the unheard and the embodiment of hope for the disenfranchised. His passion is revealed on every page and his message will inspire and change lives.

Transforming the Minds of Men is well organized and reasoned, and it introduces a new voice to the conversation about young black men in America. This book combines historical context, real-world experiences, and practical solutions for navigating the often stormy waters of you, Black, male life in America. The text is integrative, the narrative is, rich, and the subject is critically important.

McMichael uses his personal journey to delve deeply into the negative effects of fatherlessness, and successfully offers effective strategies to cope with the challenges of fatherlessness in doing so. His personal insights offer a beacon light of perspective and hope. He helps readers understand and navigate challenges and secure and relish victories. His personal examples of struggle and progress make the text relevant and applicable.

The book introduces readers to active solutions that will aid in helping other young men that are facing life without a father. He challenges us to be willing to participate and actively engage in our communities by investing in the lives of young men, particularly young Black men. McMichael urges us to see their inherent worth, value all of the un-nurtured talents they possess, and commit ourselves to saving them from the abyss of isolation, deprivation, abandonment, and extinction. He pushes us to uplift them today, point them in the direction of a better tomorrow, and inspire them to see a future of success and happiness.

The book will captivate readers. It is loaded with information, data, and inspirational messages that engender self-reflection and encouragement. Lovelle has also provided "reflection questions" that encourage the reader to actively engage with the material in ways that are tailored to them.

He also introduces new concepts that help Black men and individuals who interact with them, live intentionally and productively.

It is my hope that everyone who reads and shares this book will find it relevant, inspiring, timely, and indispensable for anyone working on behalf of the reclamation and liberation of young men, and the communities in which they live, work and play. It has been said that one cannot respect something that he or she does not understand.

Lovelle helps us understand the challenges facing our young men. He helps us believe in their potential and our capacity to assist them. He gives us a road map to not only tap their undiscovered potential, but to utilize that promise to provide themselves, and their community, with desperately needed hope, energy, and leadership.

Matthew C. Whitaker, Ph.D.
Founding Director for the Center for the Study
of Race & Democracy
Arizona State University

Principle Partner and CEO
The Whitaker Group, L.L.C.

• • •

Introduction

Woven throughout this book is the impact and effect of fatherlessness among young black men in America. This epidemic has been part of the fabric of our society for years and, with the recent tragic events of our nation, the conversation about young black men has resurfaced. In this conversation it is important to note that fatherlessness is one of the missing links in the foundation of the rearing of these young black men. This book raises awareness of and lays a blue print of how we can better rear young black men from childhood to manhood.

We can make a difference in society by challenging the status quo and having an expectation of each young man to discover and maximize his full potential. Refusing to settle for mediocrity and always striving for excellence should be the daily goal of young black men and those who influence their lives. Life and its opportunities may be challenging but, when approached properly, the challenges can be the foundation of success.

You will see the word transformation extensively throughout the pages of this book. When I am speaking of transformation, it is in relation to changing the mindset of the young black man's perception of himself and the community's perception of him. I want to raise awareness that transformation can happen in the lives of men because on so many levels black men have been misrepresented.

With this raised awareness we can look through a different set of lens when tackling the subject of fatherlessness and transformation. This is important when addressing fatherlessness and the rearing of black young men because it allows us to value the need for male authority in the home, local community, and globally.

Fatherlessness has in some ways silently contributed greatly to the downward spiral of events related to young black men. While it is not the only component, it is definitely significant enough that it needs to be addressed. This book alone is not the answer to the problem. Our young men need you and me! They need us to 1) share principles in their homes and communities so we can help them transform their mindset; and 2) teach them to subscribe to the philosophy that all things are possible when you apply yourself. These changes require a transformation – a way to change our perception of ourselves and the global view of black men in general.

While the process of transformation takes time, a positive and healthy mindset can be the catalyst to achieve greatness and change the national conversation about one's ability to make major contributions to society. No one can determine the hands that have been dealt in life. We can however, choose the attitude we have and our approach. There is work to do, and it is better when we do it together. We must believe that positive change can and will take place in the lives of young black men in America. Promise is the visualization of infinite possibilities to achieve success and the full potential in these black men.

• • •

chapter

1

BEATING THE ODDS

"There are a lot of kids out there who need help, who are getting a lot of negative reinforcement. And is there more that we can do to give them the sense that their country cares about them and values them and are willing to invest in them?"
– President Barack Obama, July 19, 2013

A long history of disparities has existed for young black men in American culture. Questions still remain about whether there will ever be a "level playing field" for black men in America. As young black men grow toward adulthood, societal stereotypes of them as uneducable and criminal undermine their self-esteem and can shape teachers' attitudes toward them.

Black men are at risk! Charles Barkley (2005) purported in his book that "racism is the biggest cancer of his lifetime." The numbers tell an unmistakable story. "Black male youth are three times as likely as white male youth to grow up in poverty and 10 times as likely to attend a high-poverty secondary school. Their test scores lag, they are disproportionately likely to repeat a grade, and they are punished more harshly than other children for school infractions.

If current trends hold, one-third of black male youth born in 2001 will spend time in prison" (Educational Testing Service, 2012). Schools often fail black male youth, administer discipline with disproportionate harshness and teach material that is not engaging from their experience. Many educational systems lack the awareness and understanding of the unique characteristics and innate traits of boys in general. Thus, best practices are not developed and utilized in a way that improves their outcomes.

These same educational systems do not offer an environment for effective learning, as it relates specifically to young black men. The authoritative figures within today's schools frequently misinterpret high levels of energy exhibited by young males as disruptive behavior. As a result, the target population of young men are disproportionately:

- placed in special education classrooms;
- suspended and/or expelled from school; and
- added to the long lists of high school "dropouts".

This escalates into a cascade of other social problems: an increase in juvenile incarceration and adult unemployment. Other closely related statistics provide even further evidence for the need to intervene. It is a known fact that black men represent a wide racial disproportion of the incarcerated population in jail systems across the United States. Over the years, articles written, speeches delivered, and conversations, in general, have reported that a strong correlation exists between the educational level of a citizenry and the number of projected prisons filled with black men – many of whom are absent fathers.

Educational institutions are not expected to teach boys how to be fathers; however educators, counselors, mentors and other educational support staff can encourage young men to take responsibility for their learning. Boys feel teachers "do not ask, do not listen and do not care" in many schools. But schools that work well with boys show that they care by listening to them (Lutz, 2008).

In an effort to engage boys in their learning, schools can assist parents in understanding and supporting effective pedagogy and influence literacy at all levels. Schools should be aware of the different learning styles of boys and empower them to feel that learning is something 'they can do' without fear of ridicule.

Having fun while learning and an environment that encourages interaction instead of having that teacher who will mark him down for bad behavior can increase positive outcomes overall. This is not a new phenomenon. In fact the concept or ideology surrounding the cradle to prison pipeline has become more acknowledged in recent years.

The educational system is so dismal, when it comes specifically to young black men, that 4th grade reading scores are being used as a baseline for planning the future construction of prisons. Poor academic performance actually creates the pipeline for determining the prisons that will be built to house the "menace to society" – as it were-- that has been created from our poor educational institution and the absenteeism of parents.

All of these elements, directly and indirectly, contribute to why a disproportionate number of [black] men do not have careers and do not become positively contributing members of society. Compound that with deficient role models, improper guidance, and forced maturity, the result is a male left to sort out how to "become a man" on his own.

So what is the roadmap for breaking this cycle? How do we believe in the potential of young black men? And how do we cultivate their ability to reach their goals? When taking a much closer look at the educational system, a number of key findings exist that should be considered in setting the stage for individual and community mind transformation and helping individuals tap into their undiscovered potential.

Foremost, research by reputable sources, like The Gurian Institute, have clearly supported the argument and findings that the educational system is not set-up for young black males to succeed. Research findings from the Institute reflect that a learning environment that requires students to be seated and engaged in non-participatory activities works well and is best suited for girls to learn, but not necessarily for young black males. This is the reason why the educational statistics of boys and more specifically black boys in my estimation is so dismal. It's because it's not in the nature and makeup of a boy to be able to sit in an overly structured classroom setting. Classrooms are unfriendly places for boys, and teachers' techniques don't work for them (Thompson, 2011).

In essence, black males are failing because the institution is not set-up to support their neurological structure of functionality. The nature of a male is to want to get up and to engage kinesthetically in a variety of hands-on and participatory activities.

At the same time, there is clear evidence that there are classroom models that work effectively in educating young males of color and even help them develop socially. One model in particular, while sparking national controversy, is that of the single-gender classroom which has yielded tremendous results.

> Michael Gurian (2014), through his work focused on "Learning through the Gender Lens," speaks about the recent controversy:

"When I began to develop nature-based theory more than 25 years ago, I did not know it would be used in all of the ways it has been. I am proud of its application in our nation's schools. Our teachers are our heroes, and they need all the tools they can get, especially to help struggling students. Among my initial findings were the struggles both boys and girls in school and communities had because the staff and parents were learning about gender roles but not gender. Nature-based gender theory, the study of gender in school and life, starts with gender brain science (the nature part of the human equation), then moves to nurture and culture; it gives teachers, parents and others a holistic way to create healthy social systems for both boys and girls."

Now, there are those of us who survived the stiff, traditional educational environments, but this occurs in spite of gross deficiencies in the system. The male who rises to the occasion despite environmental factors and traumatic experiences are few and far between. In fact, it takes an extremely determined individual to beat the odds of adversity and grow and develop despite these monumental systemic deficiencies.

Beating the odds despite life's circumstances and adversity is possible when ones mindset is transformed and able to process these life events as ways to build character in one's self that will eventually effect the positive outcomes in our community. If however, we want to reach the masses, we have to become much more open to changing our approach to how to educate black males - in particular. We have to begin to raise awareness and implement proven strategies that help all boys reach above average outcomes in every area of life including education, career, relationships, financial stability, etc.

We have to develop greater awareness and a greater understanding of the unique characteristics of this population. Then, the best teaching strategies can be utilized and implemented by introducing new concepts to teachers and more importantly the administrators who have the authority to approve the policies and curricula that are put in place. As citizens, we no longer live in a racial binary. Perceptions and reactions to a particular black male will depend upon how he is situated: class status, skin color, comfort level, and context all matter.

Whites and members of other racial and ethnic groups may also differ markedly in their perceptions and reactions based upon their own experiences in integrated environments and a host of other factors. But race remains highly salient. Black males remain at significant risk of experiencing high suspension rates in school, disproportionate levels of arrest and imprisonment, and chronic unemployment (Hymowitz, 2005). To this end, modern bias against black males has morphed into a new form. Recent events portray the killing of black males as a new societal norm: Trayvon Martin (2013), Michael Brown (2014), and Eric Garner (2015).

Many black men feel less than. They often do not feel respected and cannot compete in the workplace. Black men often experience anxiety that they will not be treated fairly in the workplace. This certainly can cause pain for anyone. Knowing that you are not respected, valued, or appreciated can determine how one will respond/react to these perceptions. Race triggers powerful emotions!

Those emotions taken into the home can only be exacerbated if the mother/female in the home displays the same kind of hostile treatment. This is likely to happen if the father/male cannot provide for the family to afford many of the common comforts of life: mortgage/rent, groceries, utilities, clothing, transportation, school supplies, extra-curricular activities, and vacations. What is an unsupported man to do? Ultimately, as young black males are often considered to be social burdens, successful community-based programs like Empower Youth reframe young Black males as a valued segment of society that deserve support, care, and educational sites that are able to respond to their distinct academic and social needs (Baldridge et al, 2011). Community-based programs could also include an educational curriculum focused on the lessons taught by a father, i.e. commitment, staying out of trouble, raising a family. Could this focus serve as the beginning of the transformation process?

Young black men are lacking direction in their lives. The need for direction is so evident in ongoing research and widely observed by the disintegration of the traditional family structure. In other words, families are existing unconsciously in a conscious world that ultimately affects a young black man's ability to add value to society. Furthermore, manhood in the black community is based on social promotion, which is not always accompanied by the responsibility required to be respected as a man and the ability to sustain manhood. Something is needed to snap black men into consciousness.

There is a need for healing, restoration, and most importantly -- transformation! Problems within the black community such as mental health, inequality of education, unemployment, and negative stigma are sensationalized in the media. In addition, when young black men continue to function below capacity, this contributes to the normalization of societal views. It is important to assist in transforming the thought processes of young men, as well as transform the minds of the adults who are committed and devoted to working with them.

Until we, as a society, address the inability of professionals to work efficiently and effectively with this population, only a short-term remedy with minimal impact will result. Transforming The Minds of Men... proposes strategies and solutions for addressing the internal issues and the external forces or resources that are needed to promote accountability and responsibility. As previously stated in the Introduction, this book is targeted towards young black males, people who raise young black males, people who work with them, and the women who love them.

I define this point as the "turning point." For young men, this book strongly emphasizes the need for personal responsibility and accountability. Once you are accountable and responsible, you can alter your way of thinking and equip yourself with the right tools so you can be effective. This is true even if you come from an inadequate home environment or educational environment.

If you are committed to seeking out opportunities to improve your life situation, you may have to overcome tremendous adversity. However, it is not impossible. This needs to change! A major shift needs to occur in which we start placing a greater value on the lives of black males. Unless we do something fast – and provide tools and strategies for them to find a positive path in life, millions of young black men (who are disadvantaged) will continue to suffer and fall by the wayside. A young man is waiting for you! Believing in his potential is necessary. Transformation can occur!

It is incumbent that you help reduce the number of homes with absent fathers, participate in the educational system that teaches/trains your child, and do what you can to minimize the perception that others have of black males and those individuals who mentor them.

You are in the driver's seat! You are the catalyst for beginning the process of inspiring hope and facilitating transformation in a young man's life! When will you take up the mantle? If we have strong fathers that do not abandon their children, the disparities presented by society become minimal and do not yield negative outcomes that become record breaking statistics. Moreover, we will see young men rise to the occasion of adversity and achieve regardless of the road blocks presented.

• • •

My Personal Thoughts
Chapter 1 – Beating the Odds

> "Education is the passport to the future,
> for tomorrow belongs to those who prepare for it today."
> - Malcolm X

- What are the current trends in the media that reflect poorly on young black males?

  _____

  _____

  _____

- How can we as a society help to improve positive outcomes among these young men?

  _____

  _____

  _____

• How can I help to improve positive outcomes among these young men?

_____

_____

_____

• What is your personal responsibility in being a part of the solution?

_____

_____

_____

chapter

2

FATHERLESSNESS

S ociety has adopted single mother homes as the norm. The traditional sense of family has evolved and even further (seemingly) diminished the need for fathers in the home. Alternative parenting styles are being accepted and children do not have examples of men in the home.

Forty-six percent of U.S. [children] younger than 18 years of age are living in a home with two married heterosexual parents in their first marriage. This is a marked change from 1960, when 73% of children fit this description, and 1980, when 61% did, according to a Pew Research Center analysis of recently-released American Community Survey and Decennial Census data (Livingston, 2014). Understandably, the lack of a traditional family structure can work on the psyche of a child as he compares his home environment to that of his peers.

Unaddressed or avoided altogether, it is not always easy for mothers, family members, and other adults to explain to a young male why his father does not live in the home, and why his family structure may be different from his peers and school mates.

Yet, the impact can be much more detrimental to young boys because they lack critical thinking and social skills to help them deal with family crises. It is helpful to remember that the separation of black fathers from their families in America began when blacks were enslaved over 400 years ago. Separation then was by force. The dismantling of the black family was an intentional design that continues to influence the population (Hymowitz, 2005). This separation impacts the behavior of young black males.

Black males have been greatly impacted by the absence of the father from his family. Osborne and McLanahan (2007) found that the absent father was a factor in delinquency, schizophrenia, sexual identification and related issues with black males. Without a father in the home, young black males have a higher incidence of drug abuse, dropping out of school, crime, delinquency, and teen pregnancy. According to statistics from The Fatherless Generation blog,

> -70% of youths in state-operated institutions come from fatherless homes – 9 times the average (U.S. Dept of Justice);
>
> -85% of all children who show behavior disorders come

from fatherless homes – 20 times the average (Center for Disease Control);

-71% of all high school dropouts come from fatherless homes

– 9 times the average (National Principals Association Report);

-71% of pregnant teenagers lack a father (U.S. Department of Health and Human Services Press Release);

-63% of youth suicides are from fatherless homes (US Dept. Of Health/Census) – 5 times the average;

-90% of all homeless and runaway children are from fatherless homes – 32 times the average; and

-90% of homeless and runaway children are from fatherless homes (US D.H.H.S., Bureau of the Census).

The impact of fatherlessness is great and has lasting effects beyond emotional trauma. In Who's Your Daddy... (2013), a podcast, the participants concluded that the absence of fathers leads to a lack of responsibility on behalf black adolescents increases the likelihood of black males getting into gangs.

The harsh reality of the absent father in the majority of households in America is a tough pill to swallow. However, black youth cannot use this reality as an excuse to settle for mediocrity. Against all odds, they must strive for success and pursue their dreams.

Maslow's Hierarchy of Needs

Maslow's paradigm presents a visual way of understanding behavior. In his research about human behavior, he purported that human behaviors can be categorized into two groupings: deficiency needs and growth needs. An individual is ready to act on the growth needs if and only if the deficiency needs have been met (Huitt, 2007). Within the deficiency needs, each lower need must be met before moving to the next higher level.

Maslow's Hierarchy of Needs states that, unless one's basic needs are met, one cannot focus on the higher needs. It is nearly impossible. Therefore, when young men do not have the basics that they need, it is difficult to experience mind transformation and nearly impossible to focus on self-actualization or reaching their full potential.

A father's perspective and presence during these developmental stages is critical to the formation of the life's purpose and direction of a young child especially boys. Having the assurance and security from a father provides a confidence that cannot be described. In fact, when a father is absent, it is to the detriment of the child as appropriate modeling is hindered.

Fulfilling the basic levels of Maslow's hierarchy of needs is even more challenging for black males in America because there are no clear, definitive Rites of Passage. The responsibility of growing from boys to men is rarely if ever discussed. Parents are only doing the best they can with what few tools and strategies they have acquired. They are only operating from what they know and have learned - even if their knowledge base is very limited.

In light of this, many young black men in the United States are living in a survival mode. Their mindset and perspective on life are limited to day-to-day experiences – not long term perspectives. There, nonetheless, are underlying factors that contribute to this type of behavior, and even more, to stunted growth.

One primary factor is that of "parental neglect" which manifests itself in a variety of forms (lack of nurturance; lack of emotional support; lack of parental bonding; food deprivation; unstable living environment/living arrangements and so on). Much more broadly, as humans, there are basic needs that must first be met for survival before one can then experience the highest quality of life.

The false assumption can be made that having both parents in the home will ensure the success of young black males into mature black men. While having both parents physically present in the home is ideal, their presence alone does not necessarily mean that they are emotionally and mentally present. It does not mean that they are providing their child with the direction, instruction and guidance he needs.

A father may be a great provider but not a great nurturer. A mother may be a great nurturer but sets poor boundaries as an authority figure. Being physically present in the home is one aspect of the presence of a father.

Being emotionally and mentally present – demonstrating love and concern for family and genuinely engaged in healthy dialogue with family – is just as necessary. The three in concert help to cultivate a mindset in young black men that will help them not only grow socially but maturate holistically.

The question still remains: What do you tell a young black male whose father has abandoned him? It is a perplexing challenge. The mother may recognize the importance of telling a positive narrative, while also telling the truth. But how can both narratives co-exist with questions like, "Why does everyone else have a daddy and I don't?" "Why did daddy leave?" "Will daddy ever want to meet me or see me?"

Even if a black child does not ask these questions out loud, he is likely wondering about that "enigma" named father – or rather, that person whom he will never call father.
As intimated in this chapter, one of the greatest problems facing the black community is fatherlessness. Every child needs a father, and no one needs him more than a young black male. So where does one go to address the disparities?

Should the black community continue to discuss privately the issue of absenteeism among black fathers? Or is it time to bring other people into the conversation? This book raises awareness to the dynamics surrounding the problem of mentoring, self-discovery, and learning to deal with rejection.

As we mentor young black males, we must stay focused on the goal to help them believe in their own potential and provide examples of what success looks like. Mark Merrill (2010) put it best, "[Boys] need to see what it means to live as a man. Men are different in a variety of ways. Boys who see man-stuff in action around the home on a day-to-day basis are at an advantage to be better equipped to be successful."

Father-Son Bond

The father-son bond is critically important given every child has a father and a mother, even if a child is conceived through artificial insemination. Father, mother, and the family have historically represented the initial training ground where social behavior and interactions are learned and developed.

Thus, fathers, as part of this innate family unit, have a responsibility to help their children, especially their sons, learn to exist and fully function in our broader society and the world. If that father is living and able, he needs to cultivate that for his sons. Part of this responsibility entails helping sons learn to develop healthy professional, casual and intimate relationships, while developing self-awareness and learning to be responsible fathers and husbands themselves.

The strength of father-son bonds in America is rapidly dwindling as a result of negative factors that impede the formation of these bonds, i.e. factors such as divorce, incarceration, and intentional exclusion of fathers when their relationship with the mother ends to name a few. Many times, as a result of unhealthy relationships established with the "baby mama," it adversely affects the father's involvement in the rearing of their children -- sons in particular.

Technology has also made our understanding of the value of relationships much more difficult. For example, technology has replaced much of the need for relationships.

Less and less of American culture and society are built around cultivating human relationships. Instead relationships are increasingly being built on disconnection from others and disengagement. Many young black males are very knowledgeable about technology because they are constantly bombarded with social media, videogames and other similar devices.

This is reflective of the way the world is changing. It clearly discourages human contact. The saturation of our homes with personal gadgets, video games and social media is a prime example of this. A trend now exists where parents buy their children video games without also emphasizing and teaching the importance of social skills and human relatability. Thus, young people are more inclined to master things associated with technology, rather than simple social skills such as how to be polite and build rapport. They do not master the use of common manners, and this makes relationship-building extremely difficult when they are forced to engage. Young men who learn how to master video games and lack social skills do not have the social skills to perform appropriately, which creates and further feeds the global stigma of the ignorance of the black male.

Today, it is of even greater importance that we teach young people to be multi-faceted in building-relationships, particularly in dealing with people who communicate from a basis of stereotypes and a judgmental perception of them based on their race or socioeconomic status. This will only be possible if we, as a community, envision our role as leaders instructing our young people to navigate any stereotypes and achieve goals regardless of the conditions and limitations of their environment.

As leaders in the community, we must instill in black males a sense of self-confidence and self-worth, whereby they will not be distracted or intimidated by what people perceive of them (as so-called minorities). We must also help them develop a sense of awareness about who they are – their strengths, their areas of opportunity and how they can motivate themselves to reach their full potential.

Mentoring programs offer an alternative avenue for simulating a father-son bond and are being used on a wide-scale basis. These programs have become a trend as fathers are not present in the home.

Additionally, these programs have helped to form an evidence-based model for improving the outcomes of young men who would normally become a statistic. The epidemic of the "fatherless generation" will not be solved overnight. As such, it is imperative that the men in the community and other interested stakeholders assume a leader-role in addressing and arresting the problem of absenteeism of fathers on a local level, with the goal of reclaiming black males globally.

It is equally important that those individuals who are stepping up to the plate equip themselves to appropriately address the needs of this generation. If young men are not approached correctly, it could discourage the involvement of qualified mentors. It is also important that organizations working with young black men understand that relationship-building is one of the most essential skills in the development and success of true manhood.

A real man must possess the ability to develop and maintain solid, working relationships with his family and in his dealings with others outside the home.

He must learn to facilitate and negotiate business transactions so his family has a place to live, has dependable transportation, and other necessities and conveniences they need to maintain a comfortable standard of living.

Numerous long-standing mentoring programs exist across the United States that focus on mentoring young men. Such programs include Boys and Girls Clubs of America, Boys to Men Foundation, Big Brothers Big Sisters of America, various fraternities, and most recently sororities. In 2014, President Barack Obama started My Brother's Keeper, a national initiative aimed at mentoring young men.

Through this program, the President has issued a "Call to Action" for mayors across the country to pledge to galvanize all available resources in their city to tackle the epidemic of boys and young men of color (from childhood to adulthood) who need positive role models and surrogate fathers. The goal is to produce more young men of color who graduate high school and go to college, enroll in trade school or the military rather than drop out of high school or become incarcerated.

While mentoring efforts are being mobilized, it is important for individuals who are a part of promoting and volunteering for these organizations receive the proper training. Otherwise their involvement with boys and young men could be detrimental and negatively influence them. A mentor's mind must be transformed in order to help young men maximize undeveloped potential.

Such mentoring programs would not be needed if fathers were more involved. How do fathers become more engaged with their sons from early childhood so that they are not displaced in the educational system, the community and the professional world? The answer is simple: Help fathers make the critical, intentional decision to be present. Fathers must work through adversities in order to remain a contending force in the life of their son. Mothers must understand and respect the role of the father and involve them in the parenting process, regardless of any personal conflicts or emotional baggage.

Instead of finding fault, it is important to find solutions. This may mean that fathers must be cultivated by a mentor in order to effectively parent, but they must have the option.

Stepping up to the plate for fathers is imperative because fatherhood is a lifetime responsibility. Only fathers can provide the insight and wisdom that their sons are seeking and need as they traverse different stages of life from childhood to manhood to adulthood. Fathers need to be fully present during the 9-month gestation process and beyond as there are critical milestones throughout the lifespan. The biological father should assume his role, with few exceptions. When the biological father is present, it saves the young boy from struggling through the identity of who dad is.

While the biological father may not be a perfect model for him, his father's presence supports the natural progression of growing from a young male to a man and helps eliminate questions of uncertainty that later hinders his self-identity. The list of skills that a male child must learn as he becomes a man is endless. So, at the end of the day, everything is built around relationships. We need each other. We need people in our lives, personally and professionally, in order to succeed.

• • •

My Personal Thoughts
Chapter 2 – Fatherlessness

> "When there is a problem don't run from it
>
> jump right into the middle of it."
>
> - Henry Schley

- Who was the "father figure" for you growing up?

_____

_____

_____

- If you grew up without your father in the home, how did that effect you?

_____

_____

_____

- If you grew up with a father in the home, what is your fondest memory?

  _____

  _____

  _____

- Though my father was not in the home, I can still be successful because:

  _____

  _____

  _____

- As a result of fatherlessness, name issues that may arise.

  _____

  _____

  _____

chapter

3

WORDS I WISH MY FATHER HAD SPOKEN TO ME

B elieving in the potential of black males is a mindset society must adopt and embody in order for it to become standard practice. Understanding the stages and barriers to transformation is key to understanding the process a young man goes through from boyhood to manhood. The stages may occur chronologically or intellectually. In other words, transformation is not necessarily aligned with age.

"Boyhood" is a stage that requires a significant investment of time and energy on the part of fathers, mentors, and other male role models to cultivate various abilities. When specific instruction and mentoring are not provided in a young male's life, it leaves a void that must later be filled, thus leaving an indelible wound that often never heals or stunts a young male's development.

The void causes young men to become stagnated in their thinking as well as their ability to be productive. This paralysis of production affects work, school, relationships finances and several areas of life that are detrimental to their participation in the maturation process.

Filling the void results in healthy thinking and the ability to achieve goals, instead of unhealthy thinking and stagnation. Regardless of what stage you are in -- childhood, adolescence, or adulthood, realize that change is not merely necessary to life, it is life (Toffler, 1970). Change is a process, not an event! A male's ability to understand how his belief system operates and how real change happens, allows him to reshape his vision from being a dream to reality, thus more action oriented.

As an adult, what do you do when you missed the things you should have learned as a young male? An option is to acknowledge what was lost and "actively" participate in the process of self-actualization and begin transformation by not allowing the void to determine the outcome of life.

The first thing you do is "own it." Yes, own the pain. Own the hurt. Own the grief and longing to be connected to a mature male figure who models and embodies everything that you desired in a father-figure. I desired that father figure, because my father and mother had relationship issues before I was born. These issues would later become defining moments in my life and self-discovery.

The only way to experience true healing is by owning your emotions and the psychological scarring you have endured. This is the journey that I have been on. I had to look at myself in the mirror many times and say to myself all the things I wish my father would have said to me. I had to pick myself up and keep moving forward – not allowing myself to be stuck in anger, shame, disappointment and disillusionment from not being able to fully comprehend how a father could walk away and change the family dynamics for a child, let alone his son.

I recall the wounding absence of my biological father that began at an early age. At the same time, I have much to be grateful for, as there were periods of my life where other men stepped forward to fill the void left by my biological father. My mother became pregnant with me during her marital separation from my older brother's father. Her husband responded favorably to the news because she told him before he heard it from someone else. Amazingly, he agreed to stay around and offer my mother emotional support until I was born. He granted me his last name of McMichael. (This decision had a tremendous impact on my life). I could have been robbed of what I consider to be my identity.

I now know that the greatest gift that I can give to my sons is to leave them a legacy, which is partly done by giving them my surname. When I was 4 years old, my mother and brother's father were divorced. In her search for a traditional family structure, she dated other men who modeled different examples of fatherhood, parenting and manhood for us.

One year after her divorce, she remarried and remained married for 12 years. From the ages of four to sixteen, there was a male role model in the home; however, in my mind the fathering aspect was absent. Not having that solid foundation of a "real" father, while only enjoying intermittent moments of stability with a "father" in the home, truly felt comfortable, though weird. This situation caused me not to express my true self. This is often the feeling that comes with abandonment.

One of the most pivotal and devastating times was at the age of 16. That is when one of my brothers, in an emotional state – saying stupid stuff that kids say – blurted out, "That is why you are not our real brother." This was the first time I heard this news. It was life changing as I had to begin to discover a new identity and new family. What! I could not believe it!

I did not want to believe it, but the way he said it sounded so true that I had to investigate. When I inquired with my mother, she shared with me the events that transpired following being conceived and her relationship with my biological father, prior to my birth. The strange thing about getting this news at age sixteen was that, throughout the years, I had always had a very unique connection to my biological father through his mother (my grandmother) who my mom allowed me to visit from time to time.

For years, she used to buy me gifts, and I intuitively felt a certain kind of adoration from her that I could not fully put my finger on. Now, this information was like another piece to a puzzle to understanding why I received those gifts and what inspired her adoration for me. My mother cultivated positive, healthy relationships among my biological father, my step-father and my brother's father whose surname I possess. My mother was always honest, direct, and positive. However, her inability to provide "manhood training" led me to glean as much positivity from male role models as I could. While my three "fathers" provided varying degrees of fatherhood, my grandfather was the most influential.

He provided me with love, support, direction, and discipline. During the twelve years of marriage to my mom, my stepfather became a symbol of what I would later define as fatherhood. From age four to sixteen, I was on the outside looking in as this was my older step-siblings' biological dad and not mine. Although there was a positive investment from him, like teaching me how to drive, my maternal grandfather was an amazing model of availability and consistency. This availability and consistency has become the core ingredients in the relationships that I cultivate.

Yet, my grandfather did not provide me at that time the emotional, nurturing component with the words, "I love you." These words were just something he would never say when I was younger. As I grew older he began to entrust those words to roll off of his lips. Since getting that information about my biological father, at age 16, trying to develop a substantive relationship with him has been a challenge and is a real work in progress.

While we maintain regular contact by phone and through face-to-face meetings, it has never evolved to a point where we have been able to move past the emotional barriers.

Even today, twenty years later, my biological dad still struggles with saying he loves me, and it still hurts. It still leaves a void within me. The truth of the matter, though, is that saying, "I love you" is just one thing I wish my father would have and could have said to me as a teenager, after I discovered who he really was in my life.

Many homes in America are led by single mothers. In these homes specifically, young black males may stop thinking that their role as men in the home is valuable. It is hard for us to visualize and fully embody manhood because we never saw it while growing up. I encourage you and remind you that your role and presence in the life of your children are immensely important.

It is not only important, it is invaluable. As fathers, my brothers and I are present in the home and in the lives of our children. This is just one commitment we have made in improving the positive outcomes of young black males who we influence. Young black males need their fathers to affirm their existence! Without this affirmation our men are lost.

My father did not receive affirmation from his father and subsequently was not willing or able to do the work of reclaiming that lost part of himself. Consequently, he cannot affirm his son – ME! For those millions of young black males and black men who haven't been affirmed by their biological fathers or male mentors, you can reclaim that lost part of yourself and find healing and fulfillment. It begins with finding the words to articulate what was not affirmed. For me specifically, I was able to sum it up in these words:

Things I wish my father would have said to me (Affirmations)...

1. I love you! (Not a day goes by without me telling my sons that I love them!)
2. Good job!
3. It's okay to lose stuff.
4. I believe in you!
5. We can work this out (together). There's nothing you can tell me that we cannot work out.
6. Keep doing it until you get the results you want.

This list of affirmations helped me tremendously in moving past my feelings of guilt and shame. More importantly, it helped me to forgive myself and quit blaming myself for what happened. It was not my fault; but somehow, deep within, a part of me felt it was! I felt like something was wrong with me. I had to get to a place in life where I no longer, consciously or unconsciously, entertained the thought that I was flawed. I could now say that I was "broken." I was not whole. I was deeply, emotionally wounded and confused about who I was as a man. There were parts of me that were undeveloped and not fully understood in relation to the world.

During the transformation process, you have to be clear about who you want to become. You, then, have to claim it. I knew I wanted to be a great husband and a great father! So, this is what I committed myself to do, not just in my actions but first in how I thought about myself -- my own self-perception.

When a man has low self-esteem and doubts himself, it's extremely difficult to reach his full potential. However, I found a way to forgive myself and to love myself, even though I never received those words from a father-figure. You also have to be willing to do the work – both emotionally and psychologically. Men, generally, are much more responsive to physical work and physical labor. But, you have to be willing to do the "inner" work. You may be able to accomplish this by reading several books and seeking professional counseling.

Regardless to what extent your growth was stunted, there is a way to find healing and a way to turn a weakness into a strength. But, you have to be willing to look in the mirror, own what you see, and then be disciplined in your follow-through to take positive action to move yourself in a direction of growth and ultimately transformation.

As you begin to navigate your way from being wounded and broken to whole and transformed, you will come to understand on a much higher level your ability to transcend the behavioral, social, emotional and intellectual limitations of your biological father. This transformation must be rooted in learning to love unconditionally. This is significant because the concept of unconditional love will be tested and applied in your relationship with your children and your spouse or significant other.

Unconditional love is a commitment. Love is a decision.

In this new life you are creating (in this new way of existing as a man – a husband and a father), you are consciously choosing to be fully present and to give your family a degree of priority in your life that you did not receive. The only way you can do this is by being transformed yourself. You have to reclaim a lost part of yourself. For many men who grew up in single parent homes without a biological father or a strong, positive male influence, we were only fed a mother's style and energy of child rearing.

Men, however, carry a different energy and approach to parenting and expression of love. Much of this is impacted by how we view our role as a husband and father. From a traditional perspective, we know and have heard countless descriptions of the roles that mothers and fathers play. The mother provides nurturing of the child, while the father sets the tone for knowing how to survive, how to hunt, how to have food in the house and how to protect the family.

Use this book as a tool for helping you discover those aspects of yourself -- man, a husband, father, and mentor -- that you may not yet fully claim. This is your opportunity to hit the reset button.

One step at a time, one day at a time, you can find healing,
wholeness and ultimately transformation.

• • •

My Personal Thoughts
Chapter 3 – Words I Wish My Father Had Spoken to Me

"I wouldn't change a single thing, because one change alters

every moment that follows it."

- Sidney Poitier

- What is the best advice you have received from an adult
  male?

  _____

  _____

  _____

- What is a quote/saying you use for guidance or direction?

  _____

  _____

  _____

- What advice will you give (have you given) to your son or young man in your life that you think will be (has been) most helpful to him?

_____

_____

_____

chapter

4

SELF DISCOVERY

Self-discovery allows men to find themselves and their purpose. It is a never-ending process. Just as there is always something new to learn about life, there is always something new to learn about oneself. There are pivotal stages in an individual's life that become pillars upon which to build. Without these pillars, it is impossible to develop young men into whole and fulfilled men. Although many men function as adults and manage responsibility without this foundation, their true sense of self and awareness of life's purpose is absent. As parents, mentors, and family members, mature males can guide our young black males through principles of self-discovery that can serve as key steps in the process of maturation from immaturity to manhood.

Principles of Self-Discovery

1.Discover Your Insecurities (Self-awareness)

Men who have not discovered themselves or have not accepted what they discover become insecure. Insecurity breeds an intrinsic fear that leads to paralysis. When a man is insecure, he becomes stagnated in the discovery of his life's purpose.

This is further compounded by not meeting the goals and objectives needed to reach completion of a task but the fulfillment of purpose. During this process, you often discover your insecurities by making a list of fears. Ask yourself, "What hinders me from moving forward or believing in myself?" Questions will help facilitate your own discovery of what has been hindering you.

For example, if you have a desire for a particular job, but have not been able to move beyond the desire, you may have undiscovered insecurities that are hindering you from submitting your resume. Maybe you do not feel qualified or maybe you feel you will not perform as great as someone you have witnessed who is currently in the position.

Or, maybe you are afraid of being successful and dealing with the responsibility of success. Regardless of the type of insecurity, it is paramount that you discover any insecurities that may be hindering you from moving forward in the process of transformation.

2. Acknowledge and Own Your Insecurities

Embrace the good, the bad and the ugly events of your life. Do not deny their existence. Acknowledge them. State their existence, so as to claim full power of their reality and the impact they have had on your life and livelihood. Do not let them become elements that make you live in silence.

3. Accept Your Insecurities (Face Insecurities)

Events of the past cannot be changed; however, inner qualities can. Individuals can become stronger, more secure and more committed in reaching their full potential. Work to fully accept and be at peace with any deficiencies you may possess. Then, commit yourself to working on those areas that can be improved.

4. Identify Your Strengths, Talents and Abilities

Always focus on the positives more than the negatives. This is your fuel for overcoming obstacles and adversity. Your compass should be grounded in utilizing your talents, strengths and abilities. Create a life vision and life plan that is centered on cultivating your strengths, talents and abilities.

Make a list. Conduct an asset inventory of your own talents. This allows you to visualize the wealth you possess.

5. Develop the Power of Influence

The more you believe in yourself the more you will rely upon your strengths, talents and abilities to open doors for you in your efforts to fulfill your life goals. Simultaneously, as part of the process of self-discovery, an individual must learn to develop and maintain healthy relationships and to exercise effective communication. Self-discovery assists in the development of the power of influence. People, inspired by your words and action, will lend their time, energy and resources in support of your life goals and purpose.

6. Exercise Independence

Allow yourself to receive support, guidance, love and mentorship. This is essential to becoming a whole, healthy, fulfilled person. As a man, it also is part of the natural process of transformation to become independent and self-sufficient. Independence is freedom to express yourself while navigating through life.

There are many men who may not realize they are insecure. They may think their behaviors are just a reflection of who they are. They may also think these behaviors are out of their sphere of control. Unfortunately, the manifestations of these behaviors are a direct result of deeply imbedded insecurities. If a man does not address these insecurities by first acknowledging they exist, this could prolong the manifestation of desired change. For example, a man may feel he has respect in the community and workplace, but when faced with the vulnerabilities of a more intimate relationship, he displays certain levels of insecurities such as harsh words, physical aggression, isolation and frustration that then play out to the detriment of the relationship's longevity. Furthermore, these insecurities and the fear of success can cause solid relationships to disrupt prematurely.

Countless theories, curricula and programs exist that specifically address rites of passage for young males to manhood. My goal is not to support or promote any one in particular. My aim is to emphasize the importance of conceptualizing a clear process and key attributes that must be embodied in a man, if he is to be defined and viewed as mature and fully developed.

Just because a man physically appears developed because he is tall and "built", does not mean he is emotionally and mentally developed. Too frequently, individuals get caught up in the physical attributes, status and material possessions of men as a barometer of manhood, rather than promoting the cultivation of inner qualities and values, such as a sense of community and family. Self-discovery is a process of trial and error. This is true even when a clear process is outlined. Hiccups along the way are inevitable. A young man can easily lose his way, because he does not fully understand the developmental process or simply lack the patience and discipline required to continue to facilitate his own process of maturation. This is why in the absence of fathers role models are critical.

My personal process to self-discovery is a great illustration of the challenges and hurdles many young men face with regard to self-image and building confidence. It was in first grade that I discovered I had the "power of influence" that I was able to get what I wanted. As a result of a crush on my teacher's daughter, I tried some manipulative tactics to gain attention. I literally would rub my eye until it got red.

My teacher would then have her daughter, who was volunteering in my same class, walk me to the principal's office to seek medical care. This experience led to other similar experiences. I had started to think, "If I could manipulate my teacher and the principal, then who else could I manipulate?" I realized that I had discovered the power of influence!

The example of progression of these kinds of behavior and thought processes over time exemplifies what happens during this cycle. For example, many people are taught to use a hammer. After learning to use it, they realize skills, abilities and gifts that they possess. As a result, they then test those skills by applying them in different environments and different situations. It was also in elementary school that deep impressions were made in my thought patterns with regards to money and confidence in my ability to make money. This initially stemmed from the words of my grandfather who always used to say, "You always need your own money!

Make money and save money, so you always have you own money." This developed my ideology that money was a necessary part of being responsible.

True manhood meant being able to access and create your own financial stream for income. My grandfather modeled this principle.Another critical stage in my process of self-discovery was middle school. I had a severe skin disease (eczema). My dark and scaly skin provoked my peers to make some of the cruelest remarks about me often right in front of me. I heard remarks like, "Ooh, look at him and his skin. It looks gross!" "Look at that ugly boy with all that mess on his face."

This obviously made me extremely self-conscious and greatly paralyzed my self-confidence. I was so distraught that I prayed to God that he would make me look like my brothers. They had silky smooth skin and was very popular because of their good looks. At the same time, I instinctively attempted to find other ways to gain approval and acceptance from my peers, as a means of survival and overcoming the verbal attacks.

I began to focus more on winning people's approval through my personality. To gain acceptance and respect, I decided I had to become more outgoing, so that my power of influence would not have to be based on how I looked or what I possessed materially.

Over time, I became a class leader, earned roles in school plays and overall learned to project a sense of confidence, self-worth and importance. I learned to disguise not being secure internally. Then, at a point in high school, my skin issue actually cleared up. So, I was no longer insecure about my face.

While I had also begun to physically mature, I was fully aware that many of my male peers were "built better" than I. So, while I had become more confident because of my clear face, I was still insecure about my body image. In my mind, I felt fat. I had not worked through the years of low self-esteem and self-doubt.

Continuing on into college, my process of self-discovery was found in being a leader and involving myself in just about any and every organization and activity available. More than anything else, attending college exposed me to a much broader demography of people. I also experienced an entirely new level of competition, as I discovered there were people who were more physically attractive, athletic, affluent, artistic and more intelligent than I was. College changed my perspective of the world and how to navigate it.

Before college, I thought success was solely about intellect.
While in college, I slowly began to understand that the success
I experienced there translated to success after college.

Getting a college degree became about learning how to
build relationships and being resourceful. I was on academic
probation multiple times and technically should not have
graduated. It is only because of the relationships I developed
with faculty members that I obtained the additional support
and resources needed to improve my academic standing. When
I graduated from college in 2000, I truly felt as though I had
discovered myself.

I landed a job working for a Fortune 500 financial investment
company. This was a huge opportunity. The firm at that time
was the #2 investment company in the country. I was thrust
into a totally different environment. Climbing the corporate
ladder was not only based upon my performance, but how I
fit in socially. During the beginning of my career at the firm,
I grew locks in my hair. One of my black peers, who was a
supervisor, asked, "When do you plan to cut your locks? Do
you have a desire to move up in the company?"

This was a defining moment for me as a black man, and I experienced a variety of emotions from anger to empowerment. In this moment, it was left up to me to determine how I would respond to the words of a peer and the perception of my appearance.

It took a few moments to sink in. I was faced with one of the aspects of being a black male. I had to make some major changes in my life if I wanted to accomplish all of my professional and financial goals. Could being a black male hinder my professional growth and development? Were the things I heard in the past about skin color determining my career true? I had to be willing to take a much different approach than I had originally anticipated.

I made up my mind at that moment that I was not going to let anything, like social stereotypes – about locks – to hold me back. This was a defining moment for me as a black man and fueled my desire to achieve success in the greatest form imaginable. I wanted to be successful despite having locks and accomplish my aspirations.

That would mean I would take ownership for being the best at what I did and not blame someone else for my own inability to move forward. Shortly thereafter, I took a leave of absence from my job for a few days to visit Arizona. I wanted to explore how living in another state potential could be. While visiting Arizona, I made another major life decision.

I decided to explore career options and opportunities outside of the silo of Pennsylvania. I made another major life decision to work on my ability to develop and cultivate relationships outside of my family and close circle of friend. I did not have the tools necessary to provide myself a stable home environment nor had I had the opportunity to be independent and on my own. I wanted to give myself another opportunity to discover more of what the world had to offer and my ability to make decisions and transition without consulting my parents and mentors.

I needed to discover life and the dormant purpose within me. Often during this process, it is was important to make sacrifices. When sacrifices are made early in life it helps prevent future regrets. Taking a risk is a great characteristic to have in self-discovery.

I packed up my life and moved from Philadelphia, Pennsylvania to Tucson, Arizona. While I had decided to venture out, I kept my job. I simply took a temporary leave of absence to allow myself time to think things through. This would eventually lead to my decision to move, but I was taught not to put all my eggs in one basket. This leave of absence served as a buffer during my exploration of life's options. Self-discovery requires being able to make life changing decisions that may alter the path you are currently on to make the appropriate detour for you to experience success along the way.

I was 23 years old at the time I made these life changes, and outside of going off to college, I had not yet established my own since of independence. Before college, I lived with my mom and had no real need to move out. It was comfortable. Yes, I lived in the dorms of my school, but this was not independence because my room came with all of life's amenities and a meal card. There was no pressure to do anything differently.In my early twenties something within me told me I had to challenge myself to grow to become more of a man. A huge part of this plan to challenge myself was creating space from my mom and ending my romantic relationship.

As a black man, I knew I had to make life changing decisions and consider the potential success that awaited me. It was important to be equipped to sustain a healthy romantic relationship and stable living environment before making life-long decisions.

This happens independently of life's influences and influencers. Living away from home allowed me time to experience self-discover and the responsibility of life. During this time, I discovered that I had to pay all of my bills, make decisions about employment, and contemplate my new living arrangements and environment. These are just a few examples of the independence I was now experiencing. A few months later, I formally resigned from my job back East.

I then moved into my own one bedroom apartment. At this new-found level of independence, I had to adjust to coming home and being by myself. Being on my own helped me as a man to further discover my ability to be independent. I soon realized the process of self-discovery was ongoing. I later in life was married at age 25. I shared some of my life story with you, so that you can see how my personal story is an illustration of how these principles of self-discovery are always at play.

These principles can be applied to any individual's life by helping to assess where you are and what stages of growth and rites of passage you may have bypassed.

Ultimately, self-discovery results in finding the person inside of you that is most authentic and most genuine. For this to occur, you must move past your fears of how others perceive you. Be perfectly clear about what you want out of life and be willing to take risks to see those dreams come true.

Unfortunately, time and time again, I have witnessed others suppress how intelligent or how gifted they are for fear of not being accepted. Instead of being held back by others, these individuals put a lid on themselves and their growth potential.

You must take full responsibility for your process of self-discovery, even if you were held back by others at an earlier time in your life. I am a strong believer that despite what has happened in the past, reaching your full potential is possible.

But, it is only possible when you begin to view yourself as being in the driver's seat of your life, not a victim of society and the environment in which you were raised.

You may be familiar with the adage, "When the student is ready the teacher will appear." It is up to you to embrace these principles and to have a willingness and openness to ask for and receive help. Break free from years of limitations – years of not knowing your true self. No excuses!

• • •

My Personal Thoughts

Chapter 4 – Self-Discovery

"The ultimate measure of a man is not where he stands in moments

of comfort and convenience, but where he stands at times of

challenge and controversy."

- Martin Luther King, Jr.

- Three (3) words that best describe me are:

  _____ _____ _____

- I am the best "me" when

- I KNOW who I am because

_____

_____

_____

- I do not KNOW who I am because

_____

_____

_____

chapter

5

MOVE

I f you are not careful, you will be stuck in your past, stagnated in your present, and unfocused on your future. Is it time for a change in your life, or has that time passed? If time has passed you by, were you not ready to move. If you are now ready, do you know what moving requires? The lack of movement or upward mobility in today's society can be attributed to how individuals, black young males in particular have been reared from childhood to adulthood.

Reared in a world inundated with fairy tales and fictional stories, many young people may find it difficult to live in reality. Thus, the reason there is a lack of movement in the lives of many young black males is they have not been equipped with the tools to manage reality.

Unfortunately, too many black males' realties have been filled with abandonment, sexual violations, and neglect. Fantasy becomes an escape or coping mechanism for them. It is impossible to live in reality when you constantly engage in fantasy. When you constantly engage in fantasy, it is difficult to navigate the realities of life because your tools are limited.

What you know is based on imagination and illusion that causes you to be impaired instead of properly equipped to deal with reality. Other negative coping mechanisms often utilized by black males include alcohol, drugs, promiscuous sexual activity, and other acting-out behavior in school or in the community. This becomes a perpetual cycle. Regardless of how much progress is made in their lives, these young men may not experience forward movement as a result of these distractions.

Any movement becomes a recurring cycle of self-abuse and re-traumatization because the young man has not learned how to use previous experiences as stepping stones for future sustainability of success. Every morning before my son leaves home, we repeat, "I am going to have a good day because I determine my success." This statement helps to set a tone of accomplishment for the day. Practice self-empowerment instead of self-hate.

Society's obsession with social media, the internet and so-called reality TV shows encourages people to escape their reality and live in fantasy or adapt negative coping mechanisms. These communication channels perpetuate escapism, as the norm.

Thus, young black males are reared in a culture that encourages them to vicariously live through others, rather than gain a true sense of self. The previous chapter on "Self-Discovery" raises awareness of several aspects of oneself that have not yet been fully revealed. This chapter is constructed to provide you with a baseline to ascertain movement or lack thereof along the pathway of personal growth, specifically as it relates to stagnation of one's movement.

Being able to "Move" is the beginning of the progress you have long awaited. When a young black man can see results, this change can ignite an intrinsic motivation that will cause him to desire and require more of himself. Simply put, "Move" may mean getting out of your own way.

It is easy to blame your past for your inability to move forward or for finding yourself in an unfortunate life circumstance. It is also easy to feel so traumatized that you feel sorry for yourself. You begin to drown in bad memories of the past and allow them to immobilize you.

Knowing your past and discovering your limits can either be used as a crutch or excuse for not reaching your potential, or it can be a catalyst that drives you forward and compels you to adopt a new mindset. Self-awareness is important because when we have a better understanding of ourselves, we are able to experience ourselves as unique and separate individuals. We are then empowered to make changes and to build on our areas of strength as well as identify areas where we would like to make improvements (Haywood, 2014).

You now have a new perspective on life and a new roadmap. You discovered yourself, not so that you can make excuses, but so that you can accomplish the things you would not have accomplished had you not known the person that you truly are. Your primary goal now should be making sure that you consistently equip yourself with tools that ensure you are continually moving forward. Never let your dreams intimidate you. Let them motivate you! From my own personal experiences, I have learned that there are tools with which I was equipped and skills that I had acquired that enabled me to achieve my personal and professional goals.

Therefore, it was not an accident that many things I desired came true after "dreaming big" and "writing out my dreams." In fact, there is nothing big that I have wanted to achieve thus far in my life that I have not achieved. Dreaming big and writing down those dreams helped create a roadmap for making my achievement more obtainable.

I once heard that writing down your dreams increases your chances of obtaining them. Sharing your dreams with someone increases the probability even more that they will come true. I call this process -- dreaming out loud. Do not be afraid to dream out loud. Write down your goals and share them with a friend, and engage in dialogue about the promise of your life. Get others to believe in your promise.

This process should be exciting. Do not allow negative self -talk to hinder you from MOVING towards your life's purpose. I have always dreamed of being a pastor, marrying my wife, being a business owner, having children, and devoting my life to the school of the better making of men, especially black males. All of those dreams have come true! You can say that those items on my bucket list I have crossed off.

However, a few more "wishes" remain on the list: a 180-day cruise around the world; appearing on the Steve Harvey Show and facilitating Oprah's Life Class. Lastly, I desire for my grandfather, who is the most influential male in my life, to travel to Arizona on a private jet to experience my accomplishments before his final rest.

Having a clear plan of action is equally important and requires thoughtful planning. Creating a plan is a part of the process in accomplishing goals and should not be overlooked. Part of the preparation is ensuring that you exercise a degree of discipline and move forward or follow through with requirements you know you must take care of. Once you discover who you are and what you need to do, the other part of being fully prepared is making sure that you do not get in your own way. Move!

Self-Fulfilling Prophecy

The concept of the self-fulfilling prophecy is the notion that what you think you become, and what you speak has a high probability of happening. Individuals often defeat themselves or become their own roadblock by not believing in themselves. You and I are not an exception.

Certainly, young black males are not the exception. With a history of oppression and the minimization of worth, the value of young black lives are inundated with poor images. This is an example of what it means to be a black man in America. The negative depictions can lead to low self-esteem, feeling unworthy, and the inability to form a clear mental picture and vision of success. Tapping into your ability to "Move" empowers you not to use your insecurities as a crutch.

Many individuals, including young black males, allow themselves to be distracted by what other people think of them and how they view them. During childhood, black males often grow up in environments where negative seeds (words) are planted and watered in their lives. Those words convey what they cannot do, rather than what they can do (Many black men have evolved from communities where no one told them they can do!)

This is a form of traumatization. Black men have been traumatized by being fed destructive thinking, and many of them need to heal from the psychological damage that was inflicted upon them.

You have to love yourself, truly love yourself, in order not to block your blessings and opportunities from flowing into your life. Even if you have already experienced some level of success in one or more areas of your life, much more success can be attained when you personally are not an obstacle to your own achievement and prosperity.

Many people do not know how to love themselves. Why? Because it is easier to look at the bad things in our lives or those things that are not going right and hate yourself. The ultimate goal is to become a healthy and whole person, resulting in true transformation. Therefore, in order for complete transformation to occur in our black young men, their view of the world and how they contribute to society needs to be positive. You have to view the world, your life, and yourself as having no limits and no barriers to what is possible.

In contrast, my grandfather is a 20-year cancer survivor. He turned 85 years old in February 2015, exercises daily and maintains a healthy diet. Within my family, other individuals have lived long, healthy lives.

My great grandmother and great grandfather both lived into their late 80's and early 90's. These examples demonstrate that circumstances could have gone a different way. Family members used the motivation behind those circumstances to be proactive members of society, instead of an excuse or statistic.

Positive Mental Attitude

Transformation requires a positive mental attitude. Success can and will be attracted to you when you have the right mental attitude, but you must be prepared to receive success. Transformation also requires a clear vision for where you want to go in life. Once you have a clear vision of who you want to become, commit yourself to setting realistic expectations and goals.

Too often, young black men live life haphazardly and do not set goals. This happens because many do not see the value in setting goals. They just go with the flow and try to live and deal in the moment! My grandmother died at age 36 of a heart attack. For a long time, my mother thought she, too, was going to die young. Without knowing it, she was programming a negative self-fulfilling prophecy.

My mother did not prematurely die of a heart attack. She believed in her ability to live life as a healthy woman and wanted to be present to see her children grow up, get married and have children. She is now 60 years old and does not allow her health challenges to spiral her into depression and a self-hate mode. Instead, she maximizes the longevity and quality of her life. She takes care of herself to the best of her ability by following her doctor's orders and recommendations.

The road to transformation and fulfilling one's potential also requires imagination and visualization. You have to begin to see in your own mind that the future you -- is better than the current you. You have to believe that inside of you already exists the ability to accomplish whatever you set out to accomplish.

It requires "faith," a belief that everything you need, all the resources, all the money you need will be provided when you are willing to work hard enough and when you are moving in a positive direction with a clear sense of purpose. This, then, results in what I call a self-fulfilling prophecy that produces positive outcomes.

This means that your belief in yourself has stimulated your creative mind to create the pathway for reaching the goals you have set and has allowed you to encounter the provision needed to obtain your goals. It all begins with self-discovery -- the foundation of inner peace, happiness and fulfillment.

When there is a clear sense of self, it is much easier to gain confidence in one's ability to accomplish personal and professional goals. This is why I strongly encourage you to make a conscious decision to invest in yourself always. Strive to leave a legacy, by investing in those things that will remain after you are gone.

Create an Action Plan: Move Forward

In my transformation process, I have learned that setting goals greatly increases the probability of reaching them. When you set goals, it becomes easier to move. In Steve Harvey's book, Act like a Success Think like a Success (2009), he implies that in order for one to be successful there is a process of thinking and acting that an individual needs.

At the same time, these seeds need to be fertilized and accompanied by maximizing the usage of your time. Tools, techniques and strategies to get moving are provided throughout this book. They will enable you to take positive action and make progress that is sustainable. Use the tools and strategies provided to create the necessary discipline -- starting with practicing and implementing the following:

1. Identify a mentor;

2. Establish daily purpose;

3. Set aside time to establish and review goals;

4. Document strategies that are going to help you achieve each of your goals;

5. Develop a list of "people sources" you need to assist you in setting and achieving your goals; and

6. Outline requisite resources and determine how to obtain them.

In order to accomplish anything, you have to know what you are aiming for. You must envision a plan of action, write it down, and then take steps to achieve the goals.

For example, if you want to enroll in college, you have to get an admission application, meet with a counselor and discuss financial resources, so that you are able to move forward with the process. Accountability may be the missing piece in helping you "Move" forward in your life. As stated previously, if you write your goal down and then tell someone, it increases the probability that you will achieve it. So, this is a very basic but underutilized tool that can be implemented. Try it, and watch how your goals begin to surface out of visualization and actualization. Get ready to MOVE!

Common Barriers

The painful reality is that many black males who have a genuine desire to Move forward in life are unable to do so on their own. They have tried and failed time and time again because they have lacked the practical tools for moving out of their own way. As such, there are common barriers that can impede their progress:

1. Limited positive role models (or lack of access to mentors);

2. Low self-esteem;

3. Lack of self-awareness;

4. Unwillingness to acknowledge, accept, and address personal insecurities;

5. Lack of discipline (procrastination and inconsistency);

6. Limited mental stability.

To overcome the barriers, we must tell our young black males about their promise and purpose. Then teach them how to "Move" out of their own way, so they can reach promise. MOVE! In general, youth and adults are often stuck because of false perceptions about life and the inability to distinguish their false perceptions from the truth. To overcome false perceptions, you must learn to "speak truth to your perception." Youth must learn to fight against negative thoughts and beliefs of, "What if I do not graduate from college?" and replace it with, "When I graduate from college!"

They must learn to fight against potentially devastating situations such as being rejected or abandoned by their father or mother. Black males are left void when a father is not present. So in order to move with this void, young black males must be shown how to fill this void with healthy and positive male role models.

Young men must also fight against sabotaging relationships with surrogate parents and mentors providing them with unconditional love and support. "Move" is really about standing in the mirror, and (referring back to the "Principles of Self-Discovery") acknowledging the insecurities so that you are not stuck in a mode of paralysis.

Principles of Self-Discovery

1. Discover Your Insecurities (Self-awareness)
2. Acknowledge and Own Your Insecurities
3. Accept Your Insecurities (Face Insecurities)
4. Identify Your Strengths, Talents and Abilities
5. Develop the Power of Influence
6. Exercise Independence

Life may have dealt you an unwelcome hand. You may not feel good enough or worthy enough to attract prosperity, love and happiness into your life. If you make a habit of practicing negative self-talk and continually hiding behind excuses, you will remain stuck (and "stay stuck"). You will be unable to "Move".

You will be unable to transform. Unless you take ownership for the bad decisions you have made and stop blaming others, there is no way you can move out of your way. I have a saying that I have been sharing with young black males I work with daily: "If you are not ready to die today, get up and LIVE tomorrow!" Take advantage of the life entrusted to you. In other words get on the "Move"!

• • •

My Personal Thoughts

Chapter 5 – Move

"Change will not come if we wait for some other person or

some of other time. We are the one's we've been waiting for.

We are the change that we seek"

-Barack Obama

- Is change important? Why? Why not?

- I need to change X in order to put myself on the right
path. In order for this to happen, I must

- I like/do not like change because

_____

_____

_____

chapter

6

RELATIONSHIP

Everyone in life will have a variety of relationships in his or her lifetime. To address the epidemic of absentee fathers, individuals who are reading this book are encouraged to raise their personal awareness and educate their community. Lack of attention to this epidemic has contributed to the impact of negative outcomes of black males in education, professional advancement, politics, and so on. The absenteeism of fathers has made a profound impact on their sons' ability to develop healthy relationships.

Relationships are essential in the process of transformation and in helping a young man to discover undeveloped potential to mature. Having friends and meaningful relationships is arguably one of the most important keys to happiness in life. It is probably the most important key, aside from our health, to [one's] overall happiness and well-being (Nosal, 2012).

How one engages in various forms of relationships must be navigated appropriately, particularly in early childhood and the formative years. This timeframe dictates and becomes the conduit for how one interacts with others later in life.

From the time a child is born, he or she begins the process of knowing how to engage with another human being, whether that is through the affectionate hug or a forceful touch from a parent or another child. Learning how to relate to others is essential because how you relate to another individual may be the determining factor of whether or not you receive a job, a professor gives you an "A" versus a "B" or you obtain a promotion.

At an early age, a child begins to develop a sense of what is right or wrong or what feels right or wrong in a relationship. This sensitivity, which is formed in infancy, contributes to the foundation for how a man engages in professional, casual, and intimate relationships. When the foundation of this mindset becomes unstable or threatened, relationships which have been formed, become unsure. They become unsure because there is no firm pretext of how a man should interact in formal and informal relationships.

Traditionally, men do not form solid relationships. We do not cultivate healthy communication in the initial stages of our relationships.

Many black men specifically lack the proper foundation needed to develop and maintain healthy, intimate relationships of any depth or substance because of the absenteeism of the black father. This absenteeism breeds a lack of self-knowledge and self-confidence, both of which are crucial to interacting with the general public-at-large. What you think of yourself is ultimately how you present yourself.

We see this with the outrage of black males across the country that cry out for justice. They are portrayed in violent ways and lack of respect for authority. Self-confidence in who you are helps you portray your true self with assurance, regardless of how you are perceived or received.

A roadmap or guide for cultivating these skills is not readily available or broadly promoted. As you move forward in this chapter, I offer several insights on the significance of relationships to the process of how males develop relationships from childhood to manhood. Information is also included about types of relationships, ways of communicating and process and stages of cultivating relationships, which are essential to a man's development.

In an effort to help black males, as well as the adults who are working directly with them in a variety of professional and non-professional capacities (mentor, surrogate parent, etc.), below is a three-stage progression for cultivating healthy relationships.

The Process of Cultivating Relationships

The process begins with communication. Communication leads to connectedness and connectedness leads to commitment. When communication starts, individuals begin to know one another. Building rapport is the foundation of communication. Rapport allows one to relate and enjoy interaction. If one of the key aspects of communication is missing, moving forward to the next stage will be challenging.

After rapport is established, trust follows – then intent. After intent of a relationship has been determined, this will allow an individual to make a decision as to whether the relationship should be further developed. Through continued development of a relationship, communication begins to strengthen, and individuals begin to allow their emotions to discern fears and potential barriers.

If no fears or barriers are present, an individual can establish a strong sense of connection. After the connection is established, it must be sustained. A connection is sustained by ongoing communication and constant navigation of thoughts and emotional processes.

As the connection is sustained and begins to intensify, individuals may be compelled to commit. Commitment is crucial when taking relationships of any kind to the next level. Commitment is the mindset that, regardless of adversity, an individual is invested in the success and outcomes of that relationship. When a man commits, he is stating that, regardless of fears, barriers, and adversity, he is willing to work for the relationship.

In the context of mentoring males, the journey to manhood is about maturation and being able to make decisions that are influential to the future of one's life. Young men may skip stages because of lack of experience, lack of maturity and lack of accountability. At this point, parents, professionals, mentors and others who counsel black males definitely play an instrumental role in helping facilitate this maturation process.

Key stakeholders need to understand that dedicated individuals will be able to mentor black males in all areas of relationship development and maintenance. One major component of this maturation process is modeling. The more young males observe the stages of relationships modeled properly, they will have images of how to practice it throughout their lives. Inclusive in the process is helping young men to understand and distinguish between "healthy" and "unhealthy" relationships.

1. Communication

Heavy consequences result when healthy communication has not been developed within a relationship. Parents who hold young males accountable and practice clear effective communication keep them from making poor decisions that could catapult them into a season or a lifetime of bad decisions.

Making bad decisions could led to choosing the wrong career path, the wrong mate, drug use and abuse, and other decisions that might be detrimental to his overall achievement and success. This is why, at an early age, children need to be taught healthy and effective communication skills so they can make appropriate decisions.

Active Communication Skills (Skills You Need.com) is an excellent tool for parents. Active Communication Skills encompasses engaging in dialogue, so communicators can practice and learn the rationale behind why something is appropriate or not appropriate. In the black community, dialogue focused on decision making is often scarce. Black parents frequently communicate to their children - verbally and non-verbally - that "You should do it because I said so. End of discussion."

This message is intended to enforce the parent-child boundaries and foster a level of respect. However, style of communicating neglects the proper foundation needed in establishing communication based on understanding. I was taught a definition of communication by my best friend. He would say, "Communication is the giving and the getting, the sending and receiving of thoughts and information, by any means necessary understanding is key, and without any understanding there is no communication." Unfortunately, in taking this approach to communication, deficits appear in the development of young people's active communication skills.

This deficit can be viewed in peer to peer relationships and teacher-student relationships to the detriment of youth. If parents are not equipping children with active communication skills and exhibiting the behaviors for which they discipline their children, confusion breeds in the minds of children. Lack of parental accountability increases the probability that the child will negatively apply the mixed messages learned in the home in other areas of his life.

Communication must be given priority as the part of the transformation process. Once an authoritative figure understands the importance of cultivating communication, more dialogue will occur when an inquisitive young person questions decisions. Curiosity is not to be misinterpreted as disrespect, but as an opportunity to model appropriate decision making.

2. Connectedness

The path to establishing connectedness for men is different

than the path to establishing connectedness for women. While both must feel no fears or barriers, men must feel that they have deciphered intent before they are willing to commit. This is the source of the renegade and cavalier mentality that many men possess about intimate relationships. Perhaps men shy away from relationships because they have not had adequate experiences connecting with individuals in relationship building. That lack of connection occurs because there has not been healthy mentoring and/or a sense of self-discovery.

However, as a man discovers himself and fills those voids of the absenteeism of parenting with mentorship and accountability, men then can begin to experience wholesome relationships - professionally, socially, and romantically. Most importantly, men are then able to establish relationships with their sons.

One of greatest relationship bonds should be between a father and a son. Unfortunately, many father-son relationships in America will not have this experience because there has not been a healthy progression of what is needed to produce

a healthy, whole man. Connectedness can also be much
more of a challenge for some men because of the emotional
requirement being asked of them. Some men do not easily
express or share their emotions and they often need prodding,
encouragement, and support to do so.

For males who grew up without a father, connectedness can
be even more of a challenge. It is likely that, if they grew up in
a single parent home, they have never experienced a healthy
sense of accountability from their father or a man as a parental
figure. This can be very damaging to the male psyche and his
self-identity. Thus, if accountability were not modeled properly
in a parent-child relationship, they apply it negatively in other
areas of their life.

In healthy relationships, fathers or father figures model
accountability. For example, fathers typically model how to
"keep your word" and serve as a provider in the home. If
young men are not provided with models of accountability,
their sense of responsibility suffers and ultimately affects
their ability to connect. This is proven by the increasing
number of men who are able to walk away from their sons

and leave the responsibility to someone else. This leads to the brokenness that a young male must navigate through when developing future relationships. If intimacy as a normal part of relationships was not modeled in the home, it will be that much more difficult for a man to engage in intimate relationships.

Intimacy in its most simplistic definition is the ability to connect emotionally. Many black males are broken and traumatized to the degree that they have extreme difficulty emotionally connecting. Many of them will actually sabotage relationships to avoid experiencing intimacy.

3. Commitment

Commitment requires a stable mindset. A man must make a decision to be committed in relationships as trust is built. Lack of healthy maturation in the mindset of a young man and an unstable foundation of communication and connectedness can lead to inconsistency and failed relationships. Any "boy" can have a child, but manhood is a portrait of how all the pieces of responsibility come together. Manhood requires commitment. As part of the process of learning to become men, males must have specific guidance in the process and stages of cultivating relationships. In doing this, they will learn about the uniqueness of communication styles and potential barriers about commitment. Without effective parenting, mentoring, guidance and encouragement of self-analysis, young men are much more likely to engage in permissive and promiscuous relationships that have little or no potential of leading to commitment.

Commitment is the ultimate level of a relationship because without it a relationship does not last. Having commitment in a relationship allows individuals involved to make decisions that not only affect the present but the future. Without commitment, decisions do not hold the weight necessary to bring about change.

Rational Detachment

Young men are not the only individuals who have challenges, difficulties and limitations when it comes to developing and maintaining healthy relationships. Many of the adults who try to help them have unresolved issues themselves or have unrealistic expectations about how responsive young men should be in their efforts to help them. Through my own personal and professional experiences intervening with black males, I have learned that the concept of rational detachment is highly important for mentors, surrogate parents and human service professionals. Simply stated, rational detachment is not taking the behavior of other individuals personally. It is not allowing your emotions to impede your ability to work effectively with young men when they engage in unhealthy or self-sabotaging behavior and fail to follow-through with mutually agreed upon goals (Treder, 2010).

Rational detachment does not require you to stop caring for the individual. Rather, you choose not to be emotionally out of balance because of any unhealthy behaviors the young men engage in. You do not allow it to negatively affect your own personal state of well-being.

So often, when parents and mentors develop relationships with young black males, they think the young black males are supposed to respond in a certain way because they are providing them with valuable tools and resources. We have expectations that these young men will automatically be receptive and immediately respond in a positive manner when an adult interacts with him. We often set ourselves up to be greatly disappointed.

Therefore, we need to learn how to manage our expectations. Otherwise, we will not completely follow through with the desires we have in our heart to help because we are afraid of being hurt by the young man. Thus, you must always keep the perspective that youth are a "work in progress" and that there are stages of re-programming and self-discovery that they must go through before transformation can occur.

Unless we rationally detach, we will not be able to understand why a young man would want to steal from the hand that feeds him. You could only begin to understand by looking at that kind of behavior through the lens of addiction. He may be addicted to unhealthy, self-sabotaging behavior. And, outside of giving him the opportunity to make a better life, the most important ingredient in a young man is realizing his untapped potential.

Until young black men make that choice, as adults, we must take it as a personal challenge to exhibit unconditional love and consistency in our commitment to relationships. We cannot give up on them. Just as parent's model behavior and plant seeds in the minds of children, we must do the same as part of the maturation process for young black males. As a community, we must persevere in our efforts to model new possibilities for manhood and responsibility.When individuals learn to incorporate the concept of rational detachment, we will learn to place a greater value on time. Time is something you cannot get back. We will be less likely to waste important time on unimportant situations such as remaining angry and disappointed with individuals because they failed to live up to our expectations.

Instead, we will learn to set boundaries as needed while remaining an open, giving and loving person. In the end, this is who we should strive to become as adults, so that what we are modeling to young black men a representation of the qualities and characteristics we want them to embody. Your expectation cannot be that young men should change completely. It is very likely that they do not yet have the ability to change at the rate you expect.

Therefore, your expectation should be that they will do what they can do based on the confines of their experiences. Do not give up on them when they do not meet your expectations. It should encourage you to say, "Listen, I understand" or at least challenge you to try to understand from their point of view. Every single moment in life is a lesson. The implications are great. They can impact future generations just as the current generation. So, if you are going to love someone, make a decision to do so knowing that you are going to face situations that you consider unforgiveable. Know that you are modeling unconditional love. You are showing that love is not a feeling, but a decision. Never lose your belief in their life's purpose. Always believe in the promise of black males!

• • •

My Personal Thoughts
Chapter 6 –Relationships

"You've got to be in a bad relationship to really understand

what a great one is."

- Steve Harvey

- What are the most important relationships you have?
  What makes them that special?

  _____

  _____

  _____

- Do you share similar morals and values with those
  persons with whom you have special relationships?

  Yes _____   No _____

- If you have a "special" relationship, do you communicate openly and respectfully? How are you able to do this? If not, what are the barriers to effective communication?

_____

_____

_____

chapter 7

MENTORING

The mentoring role has become enormously critical in the life of young men who are growing up without fathers. Millions of fathers have decided not be involved in their children's lives, or due to extenuating circumstances, they are not allowed. In fact, twenty-four million children in America live in biological father-absent homes (National Fatherhood Initiative, ND).

This equates to a staggering one out of three children. Thus mentorship has become an increasing need, particularly in predominately black communities. Young black males have been displaced in education, their careers, and their families, thus leaving a lack of modeling of the characteristics black men should possess.

Instead of mature, fully developed men, too many adult black males have embraced a child-like mentality. The child-like mentality is housed in an adult body and can only be disguised for so long, because once that adult male encounters adversity, the true nature and characteristics of his maturation is exposed. Being able to handle life's adversities and make effective decisions that affect the future is crucial to manhood.

Hence, this is detrimental to their maturation. An adult male who has not been effectively mentored by a father potentially has not fully developed in the areas that are being addressed in this book.

Creating a Rites of Passage

Successful completion of the rites of passage from boy to man is important not only for the child but for parents and mentors. It is important because not only does it lay a solid foundation of how to navigate through everyday life, but it promotes successful decision-making when encountering the complexity of life. The child must be a full participant in the rites of passage, and the parent or mentor must facilitate the rites of passage.

The black community does not have a specific rites of passage that has been outlined; therefore, this process is often eliminated for lack of knowledge. Mentorship of young men is most effective when it comes directly from the father or a father-figure. When the father is present, there is less need for mentorship outside of parenting.

Mentorship, in collaboration with parenting can be effective and cause a child to have a village that is participating in the maturation, growth and development process of the young male child. As a point of emphasis, when mentorship is independent of parenting, society's expectation is that it is just as effective as parenting. However, just as mentoring alone is not enough, parenting alone is not enough to help young males experience transformation and move from childhood into manhood.

The interface of community members outside the home has and will always play an added vital role in the development of young males into men. In African countries, the rites of passage of young males becoming men is initiated by the elders.

It is important to note that "Mentoring" is further divided into subcategories of supportive mentorship and influential mentorship. There are some black males that actually have support available, but that support is not being translated into tangible results that impact their ability to be self-sufficient. Mentoring should progress from supportive to influential in order to reach the intended outcomes of these relationships.

We should greatly desire for our impact to be enduring. If mentors are not impacting the young men in their sphere of influence at every encounter, then the mentor is underutilizing his purpose as a mentor, father, teacher, or role model in terms of reaching, rescuing and transforming black males to reach their full potential.

Two Types of Mentorship

As I reflected on the mentors in my life, I discovered that there are two types of mentorship: supportive and influential. Supportive mentorship consists of simply being a positive role model who is present in the affairs of the mentee. Influential mentorship teaches and instills the skills needed to survive and thrive in the world.

Many individuals that provide young men with some form of support consider themselves mentors. This can be considered supportive mentorship as it does not provide a deep level of relationship but provides a physical presence. It is through these efforts that young men have had opportunities to succeed and gained exposure to environments and experiences they would not have in the absence of a mentor.

It is not only important for a mentee to be committed to the mentoring process but equally as important for the mentor. Mentoring relationships are a critical component in how the story of a young man ends. This is why it is important to utilize influence to evoke the most appropriate type of change. Influential mentoring means utilizing one's power to impact a young man to help facilitate ongoing change. With influential mentoring, the questions you are constantly asking yourself are "How do I give him the tools he needs to be self-sufficient, and how do I plant a seed that he will cultivate to fulfill his personal potential and beyond? Influential mentors are intentionally instilling in him the "expectation" to have and do better.

How to Be an Effective Mentor

A key aspect of preparing mentors to be successful is helping them learn how to manage their own expectations. For individuals who do not know how to manage their expectations, burnout and frustration are imminent. Simply stated, mentors, adults, and human service professionals generally have an expectation that because they did something positive for a child that the child will automatically be receptive and immediately respond favorably to them.

The mentor feels that the good deed is the bridge that the mentee needed to transform. This is not the case. Mentees do not change overnight, nor does your good deed make them earn their angel wings. In fact, the more you do for a mentee and the more they begin to trust you, the more they will test boundaries to see if you are trying to buy their trust or if you really intend to be a life-long fixture in their quest to develop a stable mindset in their maturation from childhood to manhood.

Based on my personal and professional experiences, mentorship should go beyond the stage of being supportive. Showing up tends to pacify or put a band-aid on situations. In other words, the effect is temporary. How mentors approach the mentoring process is a critical ingredient. If the approach is wrong, misguided, or omitted this could contribute to the greater dysfunction of the population and have a rippling effect that increases negative outcomes.

There must be a long-term investment approach that includes a commitment of time and a willingness to share access to resources that support the childhood to manhood maturation process.

Otherwise, young men being mentored are set up for failure because of the inconsistent presence of a mentor and improper usage of the mentoring relationship. Mentoring relationships are not placeholders but should be a strategic form of intervention that is intended to lay a foundation, build on a foundation, and maintain what has been built in the life of a mentee. Ultimately, the commitment of time, effort, energy, and insight are what many young men need. They need mentors. They need surrogate fathers.

They need someone to rub shoulders with, someone to hold them accountable and model how to be responsible. This is why it is very critical for mentors to take their responsibility seriously. If mentors really want to affect long-term change in the lives of young men, they have to be authentic and willing to fully invest themselves over an extended period of time.

In order to make a lasting impression or have positive outcomes, mentors also must leverage each moment. Short-term projects where the mentor is present for one day is not ideal. The most impactful approach occurs with long-term planning.

However, in those instances of short time interaction, it is better to talk to the young men and acknowledge that your time with them will be brief and provide your contact information for future follow-up. Many times, the process of mentoring begins, but avenues are not offered for the young male to follow-up. If our presence in the life of a black male is to have deep impact and lasting effects, we have to remind ourselves that successful mentoring happens over time.

Mentees are going to make mistakes, and subsequently they will need access to their mentor for guidance. As adults, we need to have a clear understanding that after we capture their attention, we have to maximize all the opportunities we have to work with them. We have to remain committed to the responsibility of being a constant force of influence.

This is an excellent time to utilize the tool and strategy of rational detachment and model commitment for these youth. Effective mentors are scarce. Mentors who maximize their time management are able to make a significant contribution in the life of a mentee without having to utilize additional time or resources.

Time is an essential ingredient in the process of mentoring and helping young men discover their potential. Time cannot be regained. Time cannot be paused. Time cannot be bought. Time is the most valuable intangible gift that humans take advantage of on a daily basis.

As mentors, we must understand the value of time and encourage our mentees to value it. Instill values and help young men take sustainable action that is enduring. Teach them to believe in themselves. Celebrate progress; do not "get caught up" in feel good moments.

Mentorship, just like parenting, can be one of the most challenging and unpredictable commitments you will ever make. The investment is well worth the time, energy and sacrifice! Millions of kids are falling by the wayside. Find the inspiration and motivation to continue reaching out to those who cross your path.

• • •

My Personal Thoughts
Chapter 7 – Mentoring

"None of us got where we are solely by pulling ourselves up by our bootstraps. We got here because somebody- a parent, a teacher, an Ivy League crony or a few nuns bent down and helped us pick up our boots.
-Thurgood Marshall

- Do you have a mentor? Why or Why not?

  _____

  _____

  _____

- What do you expect from your mentor? How can he or she help you?

  _____

  _____

  _____

- What is the greatest benefit to having a mentor?

_____

_____

_____

chapter

8

COPING WITH NO

Coping With No

No. You are not tall enough.

No. You are not smart enough.

No. You are not white enough.

No. You are not black enough.

No. You are not educated enough.

No. You did not get the job.

No. You did not get accepted into school.

No. You were not approved for the loan.

No. You are not handsome enough.

I've heard "No"
So many times
That I eventually became numb to hearing these words.

At some point, I went into a zone
Fueled by my burning desire for success
And to never be shackled by the limitations
Anyone tries to put on me.

In this zone,
I learned to only hear
The word "Yes" ....
Preceding my success and fulfillment
In all areas of my life.

I still see the lips moving
Of people who wish to utter
The words "No" to me...

But, finally,

My mind has been re-programmed
With the expectation of only hearing
"Yes! Yes! Yes!"

By Lovelle McMichael

• • •

E veryone in life will face the devastation of being told - "No!" When you feel with absolute certainty that you are going to hear "Yes," it can really catch you off guard. In the end, it is how you face rejection that will determine how you progress beyond "No."

In life, rejection is inevitable. You are going to be told "No" in school. You are going to be told "No" at work. You are going to be told "No" in relationships and even during your anticipated wait of getting a raise or promotion. It is all about how you handle it! Do you let it stop you? Or, do you keep moving forward? Do you throw a temper tantrum? Or, do you compose yourself and determine the best strategy for continuing to pursue your goal?

Hearing "No" causes so many people to feel defeated automatically. Why is this? It is because they have been trained to have only a reaction of limitation. They have been trained that this two letter word represents finality, and there are no alternative courses of action.As individuals, we look at so many things in life as tragedy when they are really designed to be triumphs.

These experiences are there to help us realize that everything is not always going to happen the way we expect it, when we expect it, or how we expect it. The experiences help us understand that sometimes we have to wait for our blessings to come and dealing with an inordinate amount of adversity is part of the process.

My biggest lesson came out of an experience with group homes that I previously managed. My company operated four homes in Arizona and served hundreds of youth from 2011 to 2015. I started working in the group home industry in 2005 but did not get my first client until six years later.

I went through different phases in those six years. In 2007, my company became an Arizona corporation, but we still needed a license in order to serve clients. My family agreed to use our home at that time as the first house and made many sacrifices to prepare for licensure. My first home was licensed three different times in my attempts to obtain a contract with the State of Arizona.A number of people from my church congregation did not understand because I was so excited about my vision; however, the major plan was constantly on hold.

They helped me move out of my house, even though we did not have a contract with the state. In 2009, I finally bought another house, and the church watched me wait two more years. Without a contract, there were not enough funds to pay the mortgage on my first home. My first house went into foreclosure. It was a mess! Finally, in 2011, my company was awarded a contract to serve foster youth. My "No" turned into a "Yes" after six years of waiting, preparing, and making sacrifices. The six-year wait taught me the importance of perseverance. Waiting taught me the reward of diligence.

It was during the waiting period that I was able to mature and learn the necessary skills to be successful in business. The business was very successful. The company grew from one home in 2011 to four homes by 2014. Going from "No" to four homes in my first three years of operation was an amazing experience. Yet, in 2015, I would face another "No" that was more devastating than the first. My company lost its operating license to care for youth. Yet, another lesson in the process of self-discovery! While some might be embarrassed or discouraged by such a devastating turn in life, I was not. I took time to stop and assess my situation.

There was no time to panic. I needed a well-organized plan. Next, I went back to my original purpose in starting the company, which was to transform the lives of young men and thought about ways to continue to fulfill that goal. I realized that I could change the services of the organization to provide support and guidance to new and existing group home companies to help them prevent facing similar experiences. I began to implement the plan by reaching out to friends and associates in the business about the idea and discovered there was a need for that level of support.

It is easy to accept defeat when someone tells you "No" and start a whole new course of action. This is a mistake! When the answer is "No," this is an opportunity to embody perseverance, establish self-assurance, and create an expectation of success in your life. As parents, family members, mentors and friends, we must teach black males to develop internal fortitude -- the ability to follow through. On countless occasions, that two letter word "N-O" has caused individuals to take drastic measures to their detriment and demise. In their panic, lack of patience, and limited faith and self-belief, they will make

changes that will take them totally off course from their vision
and sense of purpose that was once was so crystal clear.

They will become frustrated and paralyzed. Black males hear
the word "No" more often than their peers from other ethnic
groups. When young black males are told "No," they begin to
function in anxiety that is fueled by fear. Fear of the unknown
causes them not only to panic but make rash decisions that
could cause an adverse reaction. When young men are told
"No," it is important that they stop, think, and implement.

1.**Stop** – Take time to evaluate what is actually happening
and assess the situation. Gather the facts before making
rash decisions. Do not panic. Do not allow NO to paralyze
you from moving forward. "No" is the fuel that you need to
accomplish life's goals. Do not spiral out of control. Do not
become a busybody. Stopping allows you to have a clear
mind when making decisions, and a clear mind lets you set
an expected outcome.

2.**Think** - The mind is a terrible thing to waste. So,
think. Do not allow anxiety to cause you to forfeit the

most powerful stage in moving forward. Take the time to visualize what you are attempting to accomplish so that you can ingrain the picture of what success looks like to you.

Read through magazines or use the Internet to find images of your goal. Then post the images where you can see them and be reminded every day of what you want to accomplish.

Write down action steps. Ingraining that picture of success allows your intrinsic motivation to kick in when everything does not look promising. The thinking stage of coping with "No" is the source of inspiration that will push you to move forward, despite life's adversities. Many times, individuals desire to move forward, but they are paralyzed by the word "No". Because they have not taken time to visualize their success, they have nothing intrinsically motivating them or encouraging them to move forward. It is amazing how a picture can motivate you.

3. Implement - Despite opposition, hindrances, and roadblocks, find a way to take action steps towards accomplishing the goal, based on the strategy developed in the "Think" phase. If you have action steps that you need help with, do not be afraid to rely on others. You may need to take a class or network to meet someone who can help your vision unfold.

Many individuals desire to move forward but rarely take advantage of their own ability to determine success. Instead, they delay progress because of their unwillingness to face their own fears. As a result, they make excuses for not moving forward. If you are not careful you will hinder yourself from moving. You will make excuses that seem valid. These same individuals fail to realize that a life of excuses is a life of delayed accomplishments.

The time between "No" and "Yes" needs to be maximized by focusing on development and investment. When you take time to stop, determine what you need, and take action, you have more confidence in waiting for the outcome to manifest. When black males begin to possess a mindset of learning to see obstacles or delays as an opportunity to learn and grow as opposed to that's the end of it all, this experience opens the door to limitless possibilities in their lives. When a person possesses this type of mindset, hearing "No" will or should only fuel tenacity in them to move forward. When a person has been transformed in their mindset and begins to feel empowered, his mind is re-trained and re-programmed always to look for the positives first.

The positives in rejection can and will always be found in looking at why you were told "No." An answer of "No" should ignite your creativity and the options that are available. This is part of the process of creating "discipline" not just in one's work habits but in one's psychology.

To believe that anything is possible, you have to learn to believe in yourself. This is why writing down your goals and dreams and sharing them with friends is so important. The more you know who you are, what your strengths and weaknesses are, and learn to forgive and confront your insecurities, the more you become empowered. You are liberated. Nothing can hold you back. Nothing can hold you back – not even NO!

· · ·

My Personal Thoughts
Chapter 8 – Coping with "No"

"It is your passion that empowers you to be able

to do the things you were created to do."

- T.D. Jakes

- How do you respond/react to rejection?

_____

_____

_____

- When was the last time you put your foot in your mouth? What did you learn from that experience?

_____

_____

_____

- Is rejection ever helpful?

_____

_____

_____

chapter

9

NO EXCUSES

H ave you ever heard someone say something like this? "I can't help it. That is just how I am!" Coping with "No" and moving out of one's own way are the prerequisites to living a life of no excuses. "Living a life of no excuses" means that you do not allow roadblocks and hindrances to prevent you from making progress in achieving goals. It also means assuming full responsibility for your life's direction.

It may become necessary to acknowledge any deficiencies that could prevent you from achieving goals and plan to overcompensate for these areas of deficiency. When you have identified areas of opportunity in your life that could potentially hinder you from reaching goals, it is important to tackle them head on.

"Learning to Cope with No" means that you have developed a mindset of perseverance, self- belief and an expectation of achieving success in your life. When your mindset has been transformed not to react negatively to "NO," you are able to effectively strategize an action plan that will ultimately lead to achievement.

This concept helps individuals to understand how one's mindset has to be reprogrammed in order to live a life of transformation and not to make excuses for lack of achievement. Instead the focus should be on finding solutions to every barrier created to distract you from attaining the intended goals.

Success begins with a dream or a goal that is based on your ability to visualize it and to feel reality as though it has already occurred. This goal or dream can be referred to as your promise. It is referred to as your promise because once you visualize what you desire to ascertain then it can be yours.

This is the power of visualization. Visualization becomes a motivating factor if you learn to use it properly. When you visualize success, your mind begins to draw a road map of how to navigate from the present to the future. In order for this to be a pathway for you to embark upon, you must have a clear vision of where you want to ultimately end up. Despite road blocks, do not let them deter you from staying on course.

Once you have a glimpse of what you desire to accomplish, do the following:

1. Write down your goals and dreams (Promise). Remember the principle of starting with the end in mind. This is a crucial first step.

2. Share your Promise with a friend. Remember writing them down and sharing them increases the probability of achieving them.

3. Take the time daily to meditate on what you wrote and have spoken in #1 and #2. You should also develop the habit of visualizing your goals being actualized. Because of the way the human brain works, when one sees or pictures success, it then helps them to create a path based on what needs to happen in terms of achieving a goal. Once you see the visualization of what you want, you will not have to overanalyze what you have to do to get where you want to be.

In other words, our minds are so powerful that if we can first find a way to fully and clearly visualize success, we will automatically feel momentum propelling us towards the fulfillment of our goals.

4. Chart your path. Begin to identify what you will need to obtain your intended end.

5. Take action! Begin to do the work needed to obtain your Promise. Living a life of no excuses also means that I do not allow my unwillingness to do certain tasks to hinder me from moving forward. I may not like living in the cold, but if moving to Chicago in the winter moves me closer to reaching my ultimate goal, then I should be willing to make that sacrifice.

Accomplishment is no longer based on what youpreferences are. It is based on prioritization and making the things that will move you forward a priority. Sometimes we make everyone else a priority.

We spend our lives helping everyone else make progress while our dreams, goals and ambitions are constantly put on the backburner. Not having prioritized your own success, can leave you bitter.

Let's take a real world example to see how this principle applies. Your current job is working in an area unrelated to what you are passionate about. Although you may not like the job, you continue working in order to survive and develop a plan to reach your dream job. Instead of complaining every day, you find a way to highlight on your resume your continued professional growth and development of new skills.

Maybe you create a savings plan to set aside the money you would spend each day at your favorite coffee shop to go towards your goal. You understand and accept that, at the end of the day, it is about "What have I learned on this job?"

Living a life with no excuses is making the best of every situation. It means going to work even when you are sick. It is being places you do not want to be or dealing with people you do not like. It is about using every opportunity, person, and resource to contribute to your success. Simply put, it is always doing your best, leaving things better than you found them, and remaining "hungry and humble".

Picking, choosing, and blocking people and circumstances do not allow you to maximize potential. It only minimizes your exposure or practice with handling or dealing with diverse people and situations. We have become so accustomed to having life the way we want it that we shut out individuals who would have helped to enhance our overall life experience. We do this because we are fearful or uncertain.

As you renew your way of thinking and continue to implement steps that will help you move closer to you goal, be conscious of the fact that everyone in your path has an intended purpose. Even bad situations and people with whom you have conflicts help to prepare you for your ultimate success by increasing your ability to cope under pressure. It is about the greater good coming out of the situation.

As it relates to the promise of black males through transformation, excuses do not have a place, because they will learn from influential mentors that transformation is about taking excuses and turning them into opportunities. More specifically, it is about changing your mindset and thought process. When your mind has been transformed, your actions will be transformed.

Individuals who believe in their promise move beyond the barriers of life. People who live a life of excuses are hindered by barriers and are unreliable. As such, they do not live a life of priority; they do not make the right choices about what should be sacrificed. In living a life of excuses, they live a life of lies and may lack trust in others. To live a life of no excuses, you have to forgive others as well as yourself. You have to be able to forgive while setting boundaries. "Living a Life of No Excuses" is a mindset of positivity.

When you are living a life of no excuses, you do not talk yourself out of staying true to your vision and doing what you need to do. You win the psychological battles and find a way to close down any excuse that will prevent you from achieving any accomplishment you are working towards.

You do not allow yourself to be weighed down or distracted by the words, "No," "Because"…or…"Next Time." You always find a way to execute whatever you plan to do regardless of what it takes, regardless of how much it costs, or regardless of how much sacrifice it requires. When an individual begins to experience transformation and approach promise, he learns to use hindrances as stepping stones. He develops proficiency in using negatives to create positives.

He begins to live by the philosophy "If I do not have it, I will create it." As a father, I have been amazed by seeing my son adopt a "Living a Life of No Excuses" mindset. At eight years old, without directly teaching him this principle, he set up a lemonade stand outside of our house charging $1 a cup. He not only persistently sold lemonade, but persistently saved.

What motivated him to take on entrepreneurship was that he desperately desired to own an iPhone, which we as parents were not going to buy him. So, he decided to take the matter into his own hands. My wife later informed me that he had saved the $200 to be able to purchase his first iPhone.

This story is a clear illustration of someone embodying the spirit of "Living a Life of No Excuses" and believing that if he does not have it, he will create it. It also exemplifies that we have to possess a willingness to take small steps in order to achieve big goals. We never want the distance of our goal to be a discouragement. Aim for intermittent goals and methodically move toward the end result. Achieving an intermittent goal encourages you and ensures more opportunities for achievement. We aim for the end result without realizing there is a process to achieving your promise.

Achieving intermittent goals is very important to understand because too often we become so consumed with reaching the ultimate accomplishment that we cannot fully engage in the long-term process required. This is especially true for those of us who are overachievers. Being overzealous can actually work against you. Resist becoming impatient because things do not happen when and how you would like them to. Accept that wanting something to happen does not guarantee it will. Circumstances have to align themselves prior to the completion of any goal. The timing has to be right to obtain achievement.

As you move forward step by step, give your attention toward being fully prepared for when the moment and opportunity arrive. Remember, faith, belief and hard work are a powerful team. When your mind has been transformed and you have discovered your true self, anything is possible.

• • •

My Personal Thoughts

Chapter 9 – No Excuses

"If you are not ready to die today, get up and live tomorrow."

- Lovelle McMichael

- List 3 common excuses you make. Explain why you make them.

_____

_____

_____

- How does making excuses prevent you from moving forward?

_____

_____

_____

- What will you do to eliminate making excuses?

_____

_____

_____

chapter

10

A LIFE WORTH LIVING

"In order to maximize one's potential and
the opportunities available, condition your mind
to consistently focus on the positives."
- Lovelle McMichael

Once you have acknowledged that you have no control over life's circumstances, but you do have control over how you respond to them and if you make the best out of them, you will be able to maximize the positive in any given situation. Realizing and accepting that life's circumstances are presented to prepare you for your ultimate destiny and future allows you to see adversity as teaching tools. These are tools that can help you reach and sustain your maximum potential through the transformation of your mind.

This is a very important philosophy for black males to embrace because the educational and legal systems appear to be designed to make them believe that life is not worth living. Because society rejects and does not fully value them, they internalize that message to their own demise and struggle to find their own sense of value and self-worth.

More often than not, this leads to self-sabotaging and self-destructive behavior. Plagued by low self-esteem and lack of empowerment, many black males become their greatest roadblock. Yet, every black man is valuable regardless of the negative programming and labels often placed on them by society. Every individual in the world is valuable. Every person has a life worth living.

Believing in the potential of black males to achieve positive outcomes in life affirms the value of the lives of these young men. This book affirms that young black men, as well as adults, who have been broken, abused and traumatized can be made whole again. They can be restored. There is a path to healing. Communities must come together to save our next generation.

Throughout this book, you have been introduced to and reminded that the resources to support and uplift black males are available. Individuals who are committed to "the promise" simply need to re-educate and equip themselves with the tools to effectively engage young black males. Communities must be willing to reassess the effectiveness of current interventions. If the interventions are not adequately addressing the needs of these youth as effectively as they want or need them to be, helping partners must be willing to open themselves to new and improved alternatives. Community interventions must continue to inspire, encourage and facilitate a process for youth to move forward, transform, and believe in the promise within them.

You must believe that every life is worth living, and despite any shortcomings, everyone can adapt and learn. Regardless of where youth find themselves on the spectrum of deficiencies and unmet needs, you can still help them overcome, move forward and thrive. As long as young black men learn to stop blaming their hardship on someone else, they can find their life path. They can move forward as long as they begin to see and accept that self-discovery is the key. Once they start the process of self-discovery, the road to healing, fulfillment and reaching their full potential become clearly visible.

The future for young black males is clear. They can be healthy – both physically and mentally – and have access to opportunities, support and mentoring that steer them away from imprisonment and potentially premature death.

They can be led to a life path that is enjoyable, rewarding and fulfilling to them and their communities. They are able to obtain an education leading to college or a trade school, find productive employment that enables them to be self-sufficient, and build a family because they are not operating from a place of insecurity or inferiority. Most importantly, they can have true self-worth because they have learned how to love and how to be loved voluntarily and unconditionally.

There are many barriers for young black males to overcome, but overcoming them is not impossible. When there is a circle of support, members within the support system are able to identify areas of deficiency and help a young man maximize the potential of the current situation.

The members can motivate and encourage the young man to live in the present. As adults and as a community, we have to ensure that black males have access to tangible and intangible resources necessary for them to succeed and to reach their full potential. Much like the process of self-discovery, there are important elements to ensuring our black males fully value their lives:

1. Acknowledge and accept the past. Acknowledgment and acceptance are needed in order to deal with the hurt and wounds that they lived through. Life's greatest teacher is often experience. In any stage of transformation and discovering one's potential, it is necessary that young men use these experiences for growth and development opportunities.

Everyone can learn through experience every day if they are open to acknowledging that they do not know everything. When our black males value the learning experience, they will acknowledge that the experience brings another level of self-discovery.

Live Through It

The fact that young men are acknowledging and accepting the past means that they have lived through the life they are now embracing. The fact that they are able to acknowledge that they lived through it shows that, regardless of how weak they are or used to be, they were strong enough to endure a situation that was designed to cause them to give up or quit.

Even if their memory of the past is failure, they can utilize this experience and the tools they have learned in the experience to be the catalyst for success moving forward.

Learn From It

No circumstances or situations are designed to be time-wasters or space-fillers. Rather, they are intended to teach life lessons and to expose briefly the young black male to what potential would look like if it were maximized. Remind them that life happens to us all, so we can be motivated by potential and not discouraged by setback or failure.

2. **Let go of the past.** Letting the past go is not to be confused with forgetting because sometimes it can be difficult to forget. To let go is to release the hold you have on the past so that it no longer controls you or gives you

an excuse to behave a certain way. So, instead of being a crutch, the past becomes a constant reminder to our young black men of the need to move forward.

Moving Forward

Move forward despite what has happened. Teach youth not to allow life's negative experiences to paralyze them. Utilize experiences as fuel and guidance. If they do not have intrinsic reminders of where they have come from, they will never reach their final destination. Most people live in the perpetual cycle of redundancy.

The perpetual cycle of redundancy is defined by doing the same thing in a different location. In their relationships, on their jobs and with their families, young black men have not tapped into their undiscovered potential because they are stuck in a cycle of redundancy.

When these young men learn to stop feeling sorry for themselves or making excuses, the cycle breaks and they are able to move forward and begin to discover undeveloped potential. They can now maximize their ability to grow consistently and thrive in a world that is designed to suppress potential.

3. Live in the present. After youth let go of their hold on the past, they are free to live in the present. They can tackle current situations and issues from a refined lens that has been battle-tested through learning from life's experiences.

4. Believe in your potential! Faith is an unwavering belief that your prayers have been answered. The more black males believe that their potential to achieve success is attainable, they will respond more positively. At this step, remind young black males they have already done the work, and they alone dictate their ability to reach the potential of a bright future.

All of the tools for affirming that life is worth living have been made available to you. It is now up to you to take those tools and share them with the young black men in your life. These tools can be applied to your life as well. As you apply them, share what you learned. We can only teach what we know. Equipped with these tools, we can offer more than basic support to black youth. We can literally be agents of influence whose impact reaches far into the future.

We can create a future where at-risk, abandoned and long-forgotten males not only receive influential support, but have a circle of adults fully invested in the development of their lives for the long-term. Then, young black men can not only thrive and reach their full potential, they can transform how they are viewed globally!

• • •

My Personal Thoughts
Chapter 10 – A Life Worth Living

"Each and every one of you has the power, the will,

and the capacity to make a difference

in the world in which you live in."

- Harry Bellafonte

- What do you value most about your life? Why?

_____

_____

_____

- The greatest obstacle in my life at this time is

_____

_____

_____

- I need to ____(do what)___to overcome the obstacle.

_____

_____

_____

in conclusion

A s a black male, it is critical that we maximize our potential from childhood to manhood and help others to do so as well. I wrote this book to add to the conversation surrounding black men. I wanted to contribute a portion of my education, experience, and work with this targeted population to assist in how we view ourselves and how others view us.

It is important to acknowledge that the absence of a father in a home can be the byproduct of many life circumstances. For example, a father may be deceased, in prison, estranged from the mother of his children, have chosen to walk away, or may not even know he is a father. Regardless of why a father is absent from the life of a young black man, a father is still essential to his son's development from childhood to manhood. The father of young black men provide their sons with direction and affirm their sons' identity through maturation. The impact of a father is so powerful that, when he is absent, there are detrimental effects on the individual, within the community, and globally.

We must take necessary action to help bridge the gap between these young black men and their fathers or father figures. Otherwise black boys will become extinct as a result of institutionalized genocide. I know that is a mouth full but if we are not careful black men will be eliminated from society. Elimination will not only be physically by are presence but minimize the impact we can make.

As a society we need to continue the conversation on how to engage and reengage fathers in the life of their sons. Although it may take some time and ruffle a lot of feathers we must finds ways to have fathers present in rearing sons. Many times we give our children what we did not have growing up thinking that is enough and do not require the development of full potential from them. Our young men need more.

Having an open dialogue with our young black men can enhance our effectiveness overall as we attempt to improve academics, emotional stability, and societal outcomes for them. We must assist with the transformation of the individual black man, his community and the global mindset surrounding the negative perception of black men in general.

In order to maximize their full potential and the opportunities available to you, we must teach young men to condition their mind to consistently focus on the positive. In some cases, we cannot change the circumstances surrounding a father's absence. But we can be the catalyst of change for how young black men perceive this void. We can build communities that support these young men and provide alternative solutions when available.

We can also encourage fathers that are estranged from their sons to effectively co-parent or reconcile in order to provide a nurturing home or, at minimum, a positive relationship between parents. Addressing fatherlessness is essential in our conversation about the young black men in our society. Teaching these young men how to handle life adversity from a different lens will support their decision making process. We have to drive home the principle that their destiny is determined by how they handle the turning points in their lives.

• • •

References

Baldridge, B., Hill, M.L., & Davis, J. (2011). New possibilities: (re) engaging black male youth within community-based educational spaces. Race Ethnicity and Education (14) 1. Retrieved from http://www.tandfonline.com/doi/10.1080/13 613324.2011.531984

Barkley, C. (2005). Who's afraid of a large black man: Speaking my mind on race, celebrity, sports and American life. New York: Penguin Press.

C Nosal. (2012, June 28). How to make friends and build meaningful relationships [Web log post]. Retrieved from http://www.the changeblog.com/how-to-make-friends/

Educational Testing Service, Addressing Achievement Gaps Symposium: Black Male Teens Moving to Success in the High School Years (2012). Report of the ETS Achievement Gap Conference. Retrieved from http://www.ets.org/research/policy_research_reports/Publications/publication/2012/jqqh

Gurian, M. (2014). Learning through gender lens. Colorado Springs: The Gurian Institute.

Harvey, S. (2009). Act like a success, Think like a success. New York: Armistad Press.

Haywood, T. (2014). Warwick counselling service. Retrieved from http://www2.warwick.ac.uk/services/tutors/counselling/student/

Huitt, W. (2007). Maslow's hierarchy of needs. Educational Psychology Interactive. Retrieved from http://www.edpsycinteractive.org/topics/regsys/maslow.html/

Hymowitz, K. (2005). The black family: 40 years of lies. City Journal. Retrieved from http://city-journal.org/html/15_3_black_family.html

Livingston, G. (2014). Less than half of U.S. kids today live in a "traditional" family. Retrieved from Pew Research Center, Pew Research Fact Tank website: http://www.pewresearch.org/fact-tank/2014/12/22/less-tha-half-of-u-s-kids-today-live-in-a-traditional-family/

Lutz, L.M. (2008). Classroom community built on mutual respect and caring. Retrieved from http://www.ed.psu.edu/pds/teacher-inquiry/2008/lutz/pdf

M Merrill. (2010). 10 reasons why kids without dads are at a big disadvantage [Web log post]. Retrieved from http://familyminute.com/articles/parenting/general-parenting/

National Fatherhood Initiative. (ND). Statistics on the Father Absence Crisis in America. Retrieved from http://www.fatherhood.org/father-absence-statistics

Old School 100.3 (Producer). (2013, June 12). Who's your daddy: The epidemic of absent black fathers (Original)[Audio podcast]. Retrieved from http://old school1003.hellobeautiful.com/2585634/whos-your-daddy-Absent-black-fathers/

Osbourne, C. & McLanahan, S. (2007, October 1). Partnership instability and child well-being. Journal of Marriage and Family, 69, 1065-1083. Retrieved from http://onlinelibrary,wiley.com/doi/10.1111/j.1741-3737.2007.00431.x

Toffler, A. (1970). iz quotes. Retrieved from http://izquotes.com/quote/185696

The Fatherless Generation (ND). [Web log post]. Retrieved from https://the fatherless generation.wordpress.com/statistics/

Thompson. M. (2011). Why do so many boys not care about school? PBS Parents. Retrieved from http://www.pbs.org/parents/experts/archive/2011/01

Treder, E. (2010). How to remain calm with rational detachment. Go Articles.com.Retrieved from http://goarticles.com/article/How-to-Remain-Calm-with-Rational-Detachment/34290941/

• • •

About the Author

L ovelle McMichael is an entrepreneur, author, consultant, motivational speaker, pastor, and community leader. As a servant leader, Mr. McMichael is the Senior Pastor of Impacted for Purpose in Mesa, Arizona where he provides leadership for the development of all programs and services related to community outreach.

Additionally, he has expansive professional knowledge and skills in the area of male youth intervention services. Mr. McMichael previously managed Turning Point, a comprehensive, residential, integrated-services youth facility. As a leader in the greater Phoenix metropolitan community, he has been recognized and honored for his tremendous commitment to serve and impact people locally and abroad. He is a member of the Phoenix Business Journal's 2014 Class of 40 Under 40; the recipient of the 2015 Thurgood Marshall Award of Merit; a 2015 State of Black Arizona Community Luminary; a 2015 Presidential Volunteer Service Award recipient, and a 2015 recipient of the Dr. Martin Luther King, Jr. Living the Dream Award for making Phoenix "a better place to live through a lifelong commitment to creating a compassionate and socially just society."

Academically, Mr. Michael received a Bachelor of Science degree in Business Administration with a specialization in marketing from Millersville University; a Master's degree in Secondary Education from the University of Phoenix; an Arizona Department of Education teaching certificate in African American Studies; and completed two years at Fuller Theological Seminary before transferring to Central Christina University where he later obtained his second Master's degree in Ministry.

He has penned this book in an effort to assist black men as well as educators, social workers, parents, and mentors, with overcoming the negative impact faced by these men as a result of the absent father. He encourages young men and empowers them to tap into their undiscovered potential and maximize it from childhood to manhood.

• • •